The Complete DASH Diet Cookbook for Beginners

1800 Days of Flavorful and Low-Sodium Recipes to Help You Improve Heart Health, And a 6-WEEK Meal Plan to Lower Your Blood Pressure

Mary M. Cruz

CONTENTS

Introduction

Are you looking to improve your heart health and lower your blood pressure? Hi, I'm Mary M. Cruz, a nutritionist and wellness advocate with a passion for helping people achieve optimal health. After witnessing the positive impact of the DASH (Dietary Approaches to Stop Hypertension) diet on my clients, I decided to write this comprehensive cookbook to make it easier for beginners to adopt and sustain this heart-healthy eating plan.

This cookbook is the result of extensive research and personal experience working with individuals struggling with heart health issues. The DASH diet is known for its effectiveness in reducing blood pressure and overall cardiovascular risk. With this book, my goal is to provide you with a practical and flavorful guide to embracing the DASH diet as a lifestyle choice.

What sets this cookbook apart is the inclusion of 1800 days of flavorful and low-sodium recipes. I understand that taste and variety are essential for long-term adherence to any dietary plan. That's why I have carefully curated a wide range of recipes that are not only delicious but also low in sodium. From hearty breakfasts to satisfying lunches and mouthwatering dinners, this cookbook will show you that healthy eating doesn't have to be bland or restrictive.

In addition to the abundance of flavorful recipes, this book also offers a 6-WEEK meal plan specifically designed to lower your blood pressure. This meal plan takes the guesswork out of planning your meals, saving you time and effort. Each day's menu is carefully balanced to provide the right combination of nutrients and flavors while keeping sodium intake in check.

By following The Complete DASH Diet Cookbook for Beginners, you can expect to improve your heart health, lower your blood pressure, and experience an overall boost in your wellbeing. This book is not just a collection of recipes; it's a comprehensive guide that empowers you to take control of your health and make positive changes in your life.

Get ready to embark on a flavorful journey towards better heart health with this cookbook as your trusted companion. Let's prioritize our wellbeing and make heart-healthy choices together.

What is the DASH Diet?

The DASH Diet, short for Dietary Approaches to Stop Hypertension, is a dietary pattern specifically designed to help reduce blood pressure and promote overall heart health. It emphasizes consuming a variety of nutrient-rich foods, such as fruits, vegetables, whole grains, lean proteins, and low-fat dairy products. The diet also encourages limiting the intake of sodium, saturated fats, added sugars, and processed foods.

The DASH Diet is rich in nutrients like potassium, calcium, magnesium, fiber, and antioxidants, which have been shown to have a positive impact on blood pressure regulation. It is often recommended by healthcare professionals as a non-pharmacological approach to managing and preventing hypertension. In addition to its blood pressure-lowering benefits, the DASH Diet has also been associated with other health benefits, including a reduced risk of cardiovascular disease, stroke, and certain types of cancer. It is considered a well-balanced and flexible eating plan that can be adapted to individual preferences and dietary needs.

What are the main principles of the DASH Diet?

The main principles of the DASH (Dietary Approaches to Stop Hypertension) Diet are as follows:

● **Increase fruit and vegetable intake**

The DASH Diet emphasizes the consumption of fruits and vegetables, aiming for 4-5 servings of each per day. These foods are rich in essential vitamins, minerals, and fiber, and can help lower blood pressure and reduce the risk of chronic diseases.

● **Consume whole grains**

Whole grains like brown rice, oatmeal, whole wheat bread, and quinoa are preferred over refined grains. They are higher in fiber and provide more nutrients, such as B vitamins and minerals, which are important for overall health.

● **Choose lean protein sources**

The DASH Diet recommends lean protein sources like poultry, fish, beans, and legumes. These foods provide essential amino acids without the added saturated fat found in fatty meats. They are also high in fiber, which can help lower cholesterol levels.

● **Opt for low-fat dairy products**

The DASH Diet encourages the consumption of low-fat or non-fat dairy products like milk, yogurt, and cheese. These are good sources of calcium and other important nutrients, but without the high saturated fat content of full-fat dairy products.

● **Limit sodium intake**

The DASH Diet aims to reduce sodium consumption, as high sodium levels can contribute to high blood pressure. It recommends limiting sodium to 2,300 milligrams (mg) per day, or even lower to 1,500 mg per day for those with hypertension, diabetes, or chronic kidney disease. This can be achieved by avoiding high-sodium processed foods, using herbs and spices to season food instead of salt, and reading food labels to choose lower sodium options.

● **Reduce saturated fats and added sugars**

The DASH Diet advises limiting the intake of saturated fats found in fatty meats, full-fat dairy products, and tropical oils. Instead, it promotes the consumption of monounsaturated and polyunsaturated fats, found in foods like avocados, nuts, seeds, and olive oil. In addition, the diet suggests minimizing the consumption of added sugars and sugary beverages, as they can contribute to weight gain and increase the risk of chronic diseases.

● **Control portion sizes**

The DASH Diet emphasizes portion control to maintain a healthy calorie balance. It encourages mindful eating and being aware of portion sizes to prevent overeating. Measuring food portions using kitchen scales or measuring cups can help individuals adhere to appropriate serving sizes.

- **Gradual changes**

The DASH Diet promotes making gradual changes to your eating habits rather than drastic and unsustainable changes. This approach allows for long-term adherence and success in achieving health goals. Gradually incorporating the principles of the DASH Diet into your daily routine can help make it a sustainable lifestyle change.

- **Regular physical activity**

While not directly part of the dietary principles, regular physical activity is often recommended in conjunction with the DASH Diet to further promote heart health and overall well-being. Engaging in at least 150 minutes of moderate-intensity aerobic activity or 75 minutes of vigorous-intensity aerobic activity per week is generally recommended.

How does the DASH Diet help in improving health?

The DASH (Dietary Approaches to Stop Hypertension) Diet is known for its positive impact on health, particularly in terms of cardiovascular health. Here are some ways in which the DASH Diet can help improve overall health:

- **Manages blood pressure**

The DASH Diet is specifically designed to help lower blood pressure, making it an effective dietary approach for individuals with hypertension. It emphasizes the consumption of nutrient-dense foods, such as fruits, vegetables, whole grains, lean proteins, and low-fat dairy products, which are known to have blood pressure-lowering effects. The diet is also low in sodium, which further aids in blood pressure management.

- **Reduces the risk of cardiovascular disease**

Following the DASH Diet has been associated with a reduced risk of developing cardiovascular diseases, including heart disease and stroke. This is primarily due to the diet's emphasis on heart-healthy foods, such as fruits, vegetables, whole grains, and lean proteins, which provide essential nutrients like fiber, antioxidants, and healthy fats that support cardiovascular health.

- **Supports weight management**

The DASH Diet promotes the consumption of nutrient-dense, low-calorie foods, which can help with weight management. The diet encourages portion control and limits the intake of high-calorie, processed foods that are often associated with weight gain. By focusing on whole, unprocessed foods, the DASH Diet can contribute to a balanced and sustainable approach to weight loss or maintenance.

- **Improves overall nutrition**

The DASH Diet encourages the intake of a wide variety of fruits, vegetables, whole grains, lean proteins, and low-fat dairy products. These foods are rich in essential nutrients, including vitamins, minerals, fiber, and antioxidants, which are vital for overall health and well-being. By following the DASH Diet, individuals are more likely to meet their nutritional needs and maintain a well-rounded diet.

- **Enhances heart health**

The DASH Diet's emphasis on heart-healthy foods, such as fruits, vegetables, whole grains, and lean proteins, along with the promotion of healthy fats, can have a positive impact on heart health. The diet supports healthy cholesterol levels by reducing the intake of saturated fats and promoting the consumption of monounsaturated and polyunsaturated fats. This can help lower LDL (bad) cholesterol levels and reduce the risk of heart disease.

- **Provides long-term health benefits**

The DASH Diet is not a short-term fad diet but rather a long-term approach to healthy eating. Its flexibility and emphasis on sustainable dietary changes make it easier for individuals to adopt and maintain healthier eating habits. By following the DASH Diet over time, individuals can potentially experience long-term health benefits and reduce the risk of chronic diseases.

- **Supports overall well-being**

The DASH Diet promotes the consumption of whole, unprocessed foods, which can have positive effects on overall well-being. Nutrient-dense foods provide the necessary energy and nutrients to support physical and mental health. Additionally, the diet encourages mindful eating and portion control, which can contribute to a healthier relationship with food and improved overall wellness.

Is the DASH Diet suitable for vegetarians or vegans?

Yes, the DASH (Dietary Approaches to Stop Hypertension) Diet can be adapted to suit vegetarian and vegan lifestyles. While the traditional DASH Diet includes lean meats and low-fat dairy products, these can be substituted with plant-based alternatives to meet the dietary needs of vegetarians and vegans. Here are some tips for following a vegetarian or vegan version of the DASH Diet:

- **Plant-based protein sources**

Vegetarians can include plant-based protein sources like beans, lentils, chickpeas, tofu, tempeh, and edamame. Vegans can also incorporate plant-based protein powders and fortified products like soy milk and plant-based meat alternatives. These protein sources are rich in nutrients and can help meet the recommended daily intake.

- **Dairy alternatives**

For vegetarians, low-fat dairy products like milk, yogurt, and cheese can be replaced with plant-based alternatives such as almond milk, soy yogurt, and vegan cheese. Vegans can choose from a variety of non-dairy milk options like almond, soy, oat, or rice milk.

- **Emphasize fruits and vegetables**

Both vegetarians and vegans can focus on consuming a variety of fruits and vegetables as recommended by the DASH Diet. These foods are naturally plant-based and provide essential vitamins, minerals, fiber, and antioxidants.

- **Whole grains**

Vegetarians and vegans can include whole grains like brown rice, quinoa, whole wheat bread, oats, and barley in their diet. These are excellent sources of fiber, vitamins, and minerals, and can help meet the daily grain recommendations of the DASH Diet.

- **Healthy fats**

Vegetarians can obtain healthy fats from sources like nuts, seeds, avocados, and olive oil. Vegans can also include plant-based oils and spreads like coconut oil, flaxseed oil, and nut butters. These fats are important for overall health and can be used in moderation.

- **Sodium reduction**

Both vegetarians and vegans can reduce sodium intake by avoiding high-sodium processed foods and using herbs, spices, and other flavorings to enhance taste instead of salt. Reading food labels and choosing low-sodium or salt-free options can also help.

It's important to ensure a well-balanced and varied diet when following a vegetarian or vegan version of the DASH Diet.

Breakfast

Pumpkin Pancakes

Servings:4
Cooking Time: 10 Minutes
Ingredients:

- ½ cup all-purpose flour
- 1 cup whole-wheat flour
- ½ cup quick-cooking oats or oat flour
- 2 teaspoons baking powder
- 1 teaspoon pumpkin pie spice
- 4 egg whites
- 1 cup plain low-fat yogurt
- 1 teaspoon vanilla extract
- ¾ cup low-fat milk
- 1 cup canned pumpkin puree
- Cooking spray or olive oil
- Low-fat sour cream for serving
- 1 apple, cored and sliced into ½-inch pieces

Directions:
1. In a medium bowl, mix together the flours, oats, baking powder, and pumpkin pie spice.
2. In a large bowl, combine the egg whites, yogurt, vanilla extract, milk, and pumpkin puree. Using a spatula, slowly incorporate the dry ingredients into the wet ingredients.
3. Heat a nonstick griddle or frying pan over medium heat. Spray pan with cooking spray or brush with olive oil.
4. When griddle is hot, add ⅓ cup of the batter to pan. Cook 3 minutes, or until small bubbles appear on the surface of the pancake. Flip and cook for another minute. Continue until all the pancakes are cooked. Serve with sour cream and apples.

Nutrition Info:
- InfoCalories: 300,Fat: 2.6 g,Sodium: 147 ml,Carbs: 54 g,Protein: 17.5 .

Scrambled Eggs With Apples, Sage, And Swiss Cheese

Servings:2
Cooking Time: 8 Minutes
Ingredients:

- 2 large eggs
- 1 medium apple, chopped
- 1 shallot, chopped
- 1/4 cup shredded Swiss cheese
- 1 teaspoon chopped fresh sage
- Freshly ground black pepper, to taste

Directions:
1. Break eggs into a small bowl and beat well; set aside.
2. Place a nonstick skillet over medium-low heat. Add the chopped apple and shallot and cook, stirring, until soft but not brown, roughly 3–5 minutes.
3. Add the beaten eggs. Let set roughly 30 seconds, then, stirring, cook additional 30 seconds to 1 minute, until egg is almost cooked. Add Swiss cheese and stir.
4. Remove from heat and serve immediately, sprinkling with sage and freshly ground black pepper.

Nutrition Info:
- InfoCalories: 165,Fat: 8 g,Protein: 10 g,Sodium: 97 ml,Carbohydrates: 12 .

Brown Sugar Cinnamon Oatmeal

Servings:4
Cooking Time:x
Ingredients:

- 2 cups low-fat milk
- 1 1/2 teaspoons pure vanilla extract
- 1 1/3 cups quick oats
- 1/4 cup light brown sugar
- 1/2 teaspoon ground cinnamon

Directions:
1. Measure the milk and vanilla into a medium saucepan and bring to a boil over medium-high heat.
2. Once boiling, reduce heat to medium, stir in oats, brown sugar, and cinnamon, and cook, stirring, 2–3 minutes.
3. Serve immediately, sprinkled with additional cinnamon if desired.

Nutrition Info:
- InfoCalories: 208,Fat: 3 g,Protein: 8 g,Sodium: 58 mg,Carbohydrates: 38 .

Cream Of Buckwheat Breakfast Cereal With Fruit And Flaxseed

Servings:4
Cooking Time: 15 Minutes
Ingredients:

- 2½ cups fortified, unsweetened low-fat almond or rice milk
- ½ cup whole-grain buckwheat
- ¼ cup coarsely chopped apples
- 1 tablespoon golden raisins
- ½ teaspoon cinnamon
- ⅛ teaspoon nutmeg
- 1 tablespoon flaxseed oil

Directions:

1. Over medium heat, bring the milk to a simmer. Add buckwheat.
2. Return to a gentle simmer, reduce heat to low, and cook, partially covered, for approximately 10 minutes, stirring frequently, or until the milk is completely absorbed. Remove from heat.
3. Stir in apples and raisins, then allow cereal to rest for 5 minutes.
4. Stir in cinnamon, nutmeg, and flaxseed oil. Adjust seasonings as needed and serve.

Nutrition Info:

- InfoCalories: 133,Fat: 4.6 g,Sodium: 89 ml,Carbs: 18.8 g,Protein: 1.8 .

Swiss Cheese And Chive Mini Quiches

Servings:1
Cooking Time:x
Ingredients:

- 3⁄4 cup unbleached all-purpose flour
- 1⁄2 teaspoon salt-free all-purpose seasoning
- 1⁄4 teaspoon dried dill
- 2 tablespoons unsalted butter
- Water, as needed
- 2 eggs
- 2⁄3 cup low-fat milk
- 1⁄3 cup nonfat or low-fat sour cream
- 2 tablespoons all-purpose flour
- 6 tablespoons shredded Swiss cheese
- 1⁄4 cup chopped fresh chives
- Freshly ground black pepper, to taste

Directions:

1. Preheat oven to 350°F. Take out a 12-cup muffin tin and set aside.
2. To make the crust, measure 3⁄4 cup flour, seasoning, and dill into a mixing bowl and whisk to combine. Cut the butter into the mixture using your hands, processing until a fine crumb has been achieved.
3. Add cold water, 1⁄2 tablespoon at a time, until the dough just comes together. Roll the dough out thinly and cut into 12 (roughly) 2-inch circles using a biscuit cutter or drinking glass. Lightly spray the muffin tin with oil and line each cup with a round of dough.
4. To prepare the filling, beat the eggs, milk, sour cream, and 2 tablespoons flour in a mixing bowl until well combined.
5. Divide mixture evenly between the muffin tins. Top each with 1⁄2 tablespoon shredded Swiss cheese and 1 teaspoon of fresh chives. Sprinkle with freshly ground black pepper to taste.
6. Place pan on middle rack in oven and bake for 25 minutes. Remove from oven and let rest for a few minutes. Remove mini quiches by sliding a knife around edges and gently lifting up. Serve warm or at room temperature.

Nutrition Info:

- InfoCalories: 170,Fat: 7 g,Protein: 7 g,Sodium: 93 mg,Carbohydrates: 18 .

Oven-baked Apple Pancake

Servings:8
Cooking Time:x
Ingredients:

- 2 cups diced apple
- 1 tablespoon pure vanilla extract
- 1 tablespoon sodium-free baking powder
- 1 cup unbleached all-purpose flour
- 1/3 cup unsweetened applesauce
- 1/3 cup real maple syrup
- 3/4 cup nondairy milk
- 1 tablespoon sugar
- 1/2 teaspoon ground cinnamon

Directions:
1. Preheat oven to 400°F. Lightly spray an ovenproof skillet with oil.
2. Place the apple, vanilla, baking powder, flour, applesauce, maple syrup, and nondairy milk into a large mixing bowl and stir well to combine. Pour batter into the prepared skillet and smooth top to even.
3. Combine the sugar and cinnamon in a small bowl and sprinkle evenly over the batter.
4. Place pan on middle rack in oven and bake for 25 minutes. Remove from oven. Carefully loosen pancake from pan using a spatula. Slice into sections and serve immediately.

Nutrition Info:
- InfoCalories: 126,Fat: 1 g,Protein: 2 g,Sodium: 10 mg,Carbohydrates: 27 .

Avo Trout Toastie

Servings: 2
Cooking Time: 3 Mins
Ingredients:

- 2 Sesame bagels, cut in half
- 1 big avocado,
- 3 ounces cold smoked rainbow trout
- Freshly squeezed lemon juice
- Freshly ground black pepper
- Fresh parsley, shredded
- 2 black cherry tomatoes, cut into slices

Directions:
1. Gently toast the bagels under the grill or in a flat pan on a very low heat.
2. While the bagels toast, cut, peel, and pit the avocados, then place in a bowl with a tablespoon of lemon juice, and smash lightly.
3. To serve: smear the avocado evenly over the bagel halves. Lay the tomato slices down, and top with the smoked trout.
4. Finish it off with a generous splash of lemon juice over the fish and some freshly ground black pepper and fresh parsley to taste.

Nutrition Info:
- Info382 calories,37g carbs,19g protein,490mg sodium,20g fat.

Apples And Cinnamon Oatmeal

Servings: 2
Cooking Time:x
Ingredients:

- 1 1/2 cups unsweetened plain almond milk
- 1 cup old-fashioned oats
- 1 large unpeeled Granny Smith apple, cubed
- 1/4 teaspoon ground cinnamon
- 2 tablespoons toasted walnut pieces

Directions:
1. Bring the milk to a simmer over medium heat, and add the oats and apple. Stir until most of the liquid is absorbed, about 4 minutes. Stir in the cinnamon. Scoop the oatmeal mixture into two bowls, and top with walnuts.

Nutrition Info:
- InfoCalories 377,Total Fat 16 g,Sodium 77 mg,Total Carbohydrate 73 g,Protein 13 .

2-minute Egg And Vegetable Breakfast Mug

Servings:1
Cooking Time:2 Minutes

Ingredients:

- 2 eggs (see Tips)
- 2 tablespoons fat-free milk or plant-based milk
- ¼ cup thinly sliced spinach
- 2 cherry tomatoes, halved
- 2 tablespoons chopped mushroom
- 4 frozen broccoli florets, chopped
- ½ teaspoon dried basil
- Freshly ground black pepper
- Optional toppings: salsa, sliced avocado, shredded cheese

Directions:

1. Spray the inside of a large microwave-safe mug (see Tips), custard cup, or ramekin with cooking spray.
2. Add the eggs and milk to the mug and using a fork, mix until the yolks are combined. Fill the mug two-thirds full (don't fill to the brim), because the eggs will fluff up and expand during the cooking process.
3. Add the spinach, tomatoes, mushroom, broccoli, basil, and pepper to taste. Gently stir to combine.
4. Transfer the mug to the microwave and cook on high for 1 minute.
5. Stir the mixture and microwave for an additional minute or until the eggs are almost set. Cooking times will vary depending on your microwave's strength.
6. Sprinkle with optional toppings, if desired.

Nutrition Info:

- InfoCalories 175,Sodium 169 mg,Total carbohydrates 6 g,Protein 15 .

Broccoli Omelet

Servings: 1
Cooking Time:x

Ingredients:

- 2 egg whites
- 1 whole egg
- 2 tablespoons extra virgin olive oil
- 1/2 cup chopped broccoli
- 1 large clove garlic, minced
- 1/8 teaspoon chile pepper flakes
- 1/4 cup low-fat feta cheese
- Cracked black pepper

Directions:

1. Whisk the egg whites and egg in a small bowl. Heat a small nonstick pan on medium heat. Add 1 tablespoon of the oil to the hot pan and when the oil is hot, add the broccoli. Cook for 2 minutes before adding the garlic, chile pepper flakes, and black pepper to taste. Cook for 2 minutes more, then remove the broccoli mixture from the pan, and place in a separate bowl. Turn the heat to low, add the remaining tablespoon of oil and when the oil is hot, add the whisked eggs. Once they start to bubble and pull away from the sides, about 30 seconds, flip the omelet over and immediately scoop the broccoli mixture and feta cheese on one half of the omelet. Fold the omelet over, turn off the heat, and cover the pan with a lid for 2 minutes. Serve immediately.

Nutrition Info:

- InfoCalories 493,Total Fat 41 g,Sodium 984 mg,Total Carbohydrate 6 g,Protein 29 .

Quinoa And Spinach Power Salad

Servings:2
Cooking Time:10 Minutes
Ingredients:

- ½ cup quinoa, rinsed and drained
- 2 cups spinach, finely chopped
- 1 medium tomato, diced
- 1 cup sugar snap peas
- ½ cup diced cucumbers
- ¼ cup sliced almonds
- ½ cup canned chickpeas, rinsed and drained
- 1½ tablespoons fresh lemon juice
- 1½ tablespoons extra-virgin olive oil
- ¼ teaspoon salt
- ¼ teaspoon freshly ground black pepper

Directions:

1. In a medium saucepan, combine the quinoa and 1 cup water and bring to a boil over medium-high heat. Reduce the heat to a simmer, cover, and cook until the quinoa has absorbed all of the water, 10 to 15 minutes (see Tip).
2. Remove from the heat, cover, and let the quinoa steam for 5 minutes. Remove the lid and fluff with a fork.
3. In a large bowl, combine the spinach, tomato, snap peas, cucumbers, almonds, chickpeas, and cooled quinoa.
4. In a small bowl, whisk together the lemon juice, olive oil, salt, and pepper. Pour over the quinoa and vegetables and toss to coat.
5. Portion into 2 serving bowls.

Nutrition Info:

- InfoCalories 439,Sodium 333 mg,Total carbohydrates 54 g,Protein 15 .

Strawberry Yogurt Smoothie

Servings:1
Cooking Time:x
Ingredients:

- 1 cup plain nonfat or low-fat Greek yogurt
- 1 cup frozen strawberries
- 1 cup ice
- ½ cup nonfat or low-fat milk
- ½ orange, peeled
- ½ frozen banana

Directions:

1. Add all of the ingredients to a blender and process until smooth.
2. Enjoy immediately.

Nutrition Info:

- InfoCalories: 305,Total Fat: 1g,Sodium: 170mg,Total Carbohydrate: 52g,Protein: 29.

Green Apple Pie Protein Smoothie

Servings:1
Cooking Time:5minutes
Ingredients:

- ¾ cup unsweetened vanilla almond or cashew milk
- 2 tablespoons oat bran
- ¼ teaspoon apple pie spice or ground cinnamon
- ½ teaspoon vanilla extract
- 1 cup baby spinach or ⅓ cup frozen (see Tips)
- ½ cup nonfat plain Greek yogurt
- 1 tablespoon avocado
- ½ medium banana, sliced and frozen
- ½ cup green apple, unpeeled, chopped and frozen (see Tips)
- ¼ cup cooked or canned white beans (see Tips), rinsed and drained
- ½ cup ice, or to desired consistency

Directions:

1. In a high-powered blender, combine the milk, oat bran, apple pie spice, vanilla, spinach, yogurt, avocado, banana, apple, beans, and ice. Blend until smooth. Serve immediately.

Nutrition Info:

- InfoCalories 319,Sodium 226 mg,Total carbohydrates 50 g,Protein 21 .

Chocolate-cherry Smoothie Bowl

Servings:1
Cooking Time:5minutes
Ingredients:
- SMOOTHIE
- ½ cup unsweetened vanilla almond or cashew milk
- 1 teaspoon vanilla extract
- 1 cup fresh baby spinach or ⅓ cup frozen (see Tips)
- 1 tablespoon almond butter
- 1 tablespoon unsweetened cocoa powder
- ½ cup nonfat plain Greek yogurt
- ¾ cup frozen cherries
- ½ medium banana, sliced and frozen
- 3 to 4 ice cubes, or to desired consistency
- FOR SERVING
- ½ small banana, sliced
- ¼ cup berries, such as blueberries, raspberries, or strawberries
- 1 teaspoon sliced almonds
- ½ tablespoon cacao nibs

Directions:
1. Make the smoothie: In a high-powered blender, combine the milk, vanilla, spinach, almond butter, cocoa, yogurt, cherries, banana, and ice. Blend until thick and creamy.
2. To serve, pour into a bowl and top with the sliced banana, berries, sliced almonds, and cacao nibs. Enjoy immediately.

Nutrition Info:
- InfoCalories 412,Sodium 182 mg,Total carbohydrates 61 g,Protein 20 .

Summer Veg Brekkie Cup

Servings: 1
Cooking Time: 2 Mins
Ingredients:
- Unsalted butter or cooking spray, for greasing
- 2 tbsp. fat-free milk
- 2 eggs
- 4 frozen florets broccoli, chopped
- 2 tbsp. sliced button mushrooms
- 2 halved cherry tomatoes
- ¼ cup chard, shredded
- ¼ tsp fresh thyme, chopped
- ½ tsp basil, chopped finely (dried or fresh)
- Black pepper, freshly ground
- 1 tbsp. grated cheese to garnish

Directions:
1. Grease a microwave-safe mug with unsalted butter or cooking spray.
2. Making sure not to fill the cup above 2/3 high, add the milk and the eggs, and combine thoroughly using a whisk or a fork.
3. Gently stir in your vegetables, herbs, and pepper to taste.
4. Cook the mug in the microwave on high for 1 minute.
5. Remove mug from the microwave and stir your cup gently, then cook on high for another minute or until the egg is firm and fluffy.
6. Sprinkle with grated cheese to garnish.
7. Serve warm and enjoy!

Kale And Apple Smoothie

Servings:1
Cooking Time:x
Ingredients:

- 1 cup stemmed and loosely packed kale leaves, well washed
- ½ sweet apple, such as Jonathan or Gala, cored and coarsely chopped
- ⅓ cup apple cider
- 2 tablespoons sunflower seeds
- 6 ice cubes
- 8 fresh mint leaves

Directions:
1. Puree all ingredients in a blender until smooth. Pour into a tall glass and serve immediately.

Ricotta Breakfast Toast Two Ways

Servings:1
Cooking Time:3 Minutes
Ingredients:

- Strawberry Almond Ricotta Toast
- 1 slice hearty whole-grain bread
- ⅓ cup part-skim ricotta cheese
- 1 teaspoon honey
- ½ cup sliced strawberries
- 1 tablespoon sliced almonds
- Pinch of ground cinnamon

Directions:
1. Toast the bread to your liking.
2. Spread with the ricotta cheese, drizzle with the honey, layer the strawberries on top, and sprinkle with the almonds and cinnamon.

Nutrition Info:

- InfoCalories 286,Sodium 379 mg,Total carbohydrates 38 g,Protein 16 .

Broccoli And Pepper Jack Omelet

Servings:1
Cooking Time:x
Ingredients:

- Olive oil in a pump sprayer
- ½ cup seasoned liquid egg substitute
- 1 slice reduced-fat pepper Jack cheese, torn into a few pieces
- ¼ cup cooked and chopped broccoli (thawed frozen broccoli is fine), warmed in a microwave

Directions:
1. Spray a small nonstick skillet with oil and heat over medium heat. Add the egg substitute and cook until the edges are set, about 15 seconds. Using a heatproof spatula, lift the edges of the egg substitute so the uncooked liquid can flow underneath. Continue cooking, lifting the edges about every 15 seconds, until the omelet is set, about 1½ minutes total.
2. Remove from the heat. Scatter the cheese and broccoli over the top of the omelet. Tilt the pan slightly, and use the spatula to help the omelet fold over on itself into thirds. (The cheese will melt from the heat of the omelet.) Slide out onto a plate and serve.

Nutrition Info:

- Info145 calories,18 g protein,5 g carbohydrates,4 g fat,381 mg sodiu.

Raspberry Polenta Waffles

Servings: 8
Cooking Time: 20 Mins
Ingredients:

- 1 tbsp. unsalted butter, melted
- 1 tbsp. sunflower oil
- 1 ¼ cups low fat milk
- 1 cup plain cake flour
- 2 tbsp. caster sugar
- 1 cup finely ground polenta
- 1 ½ tsp baking powder
- 2 large egg whites
- 2 cups low fat, plain yogurt
- 6 ounces raspberries, for serving
- Sunflower oil in a spray bottle for the waffle iron

Directions:

1. Mix the milk, oil, and melted butter together in a bowl.
2. Sift the flour, sugar, polenta, and baking powder into a separate bowl, whisk gently, then stir in the milk mixture until just combined. Set aside.
3. Set the oven to 200ºF to preheat and turn on your waffle iron to warm up.
4. In an electric mixer, whisk the egg whites until stiff peaks form. Gently fold ⅔ of the egg whites into the flour mixture, add the last ⅓ and fold in.
5. Oil the waffle iron lightly, and then add about 1 cup of the waffle batter into the iron. Close and let cook until they are golden brown and cooked through.
6. To serve, place 2 waffles on a plate stacked on top of each other. Spoon ¼ cup yogurt over them and cascade a handful of raspberries over the top.
7. Enjoy warm!

Nutrition Info:

- Info233 calories,38g carbs,9g protein,239mg sodium,5g fat.

Pumpkin Waffles

Servings:6
Cooking Time:x
Ingredients:

- 1 cup pumpkin purée
- 1 cup white whole-wheat flour
- 1/2 cup unbleached all-purpose flour
- 1/3 cup brown sugar
- 11/2 cups low-fat milk
- 1 egg white
- 1 tablespoon canola oil
- 1 tablespoon sodium-free baking powder
- 1 tablespoon pure vanilla extract
- 2 teaspoons ground cinnamon
- 1/4 teaspoon ground allspice
- 1/4 teaspoon ground ginger

Directions:

1. Measure ingredients into a large mixing bowl and beat until smooth.
2. Heat waffle iron. Spray lightly with oil, then ladle batter onto the hot surface, being careful to avoid the edges (batter will spread once appliance is closed). Close waffle iron and bake until golden brown, roughly 4–5 minutes.
3. Remove baked waffles from iron and repeat process with remaining batter. Serve immediately.

Nutrition Info:

- InfoCalories: 219,Fat: 3 g,Protein: 7 g,Sodium: 43 mg,Carbohydrates: 41 .

Appetizers, Snacks And Side Dishes

Grilled Rustic Corn

Servings: 4
Cooking Time:x
Ingredients:

- 4 large ears of corn
- 1/4 teaspoon sea salt
- 1/4 teaspoon cracked black pepper
- 4 tablespoons extra virgin olive oil
- 4 large cloves garlic, minced finely

Directions:

1. Peel back the husks and remove the silk from each ear of corn. Mix the salt and pepper together in a small bowl. Brush the kernels with oil, and sprinkle each with minced garlic and then the salt and pepper mixture. Fold the husks back over the corn, and grill over low heat until cooked through, 12 to 15 minutes, turning occasionally.

Nutrition Info:

- InfoCalories 249,Total Fat 16 g,Sodium 167 mg,Total Carbohydrate 28 g,Protein 5 .

Apple Walnut Wheat Stuffing

Servings:8
Cooking Time:x
Ingredients:

- 1 tablespoon olive oil
- 3 cloves garlic, minced
- 1 large onion, chopped
- 3 medium tart green apples, diced
- 4 cups cubed salt-free wheat bread
- 3⁄4 cup low-sodium chicken broth
- 1⁄2 cup chopped walnuts
- 1 tablespoon freshly squeezed lemon juice
- 1 tablespoon brown sugar
- 11⁄2 teaspoons ground cinnamon
- 1⁄2 teaspoon freshly ground black pepper
- 1⁄4 teaspoon ground nutmeg

Directions:

1. Preheat oven to 325°F. Spray a lidded baking pan lightly with oil and set aside.
2. Heat the oil in a large sauté pan over medium. Add the garlic and onion and sauté for 2 minutes. Remove pan from heat.
3. Add the remaining ingredients and stir gently to combine.
4. Spread mixture in pan, cover, and place on middle rack in oven. Bake for 20 minutes.
5. Uncover and bake another 10 minutes. Remove from oven and serve immediately.

Nutrition Info:

- InfoCalories: 158,Fat: 7 g,Protein: 3 g,Sodium: 13 mg,Carbohydrates: 22 .

Cauliflower Mashed "potatoes"

Servings:4
Cooking Time: 10 Minutes
Ingredients:

- 16 cups water (enough to cover cauliflower)
- 1 head cauliflower, trimmed and cut into florets
- 4 garlic cloves
- 1 tablespoon olive oil
- ¼ teaspoon salt
- ⅛ teaspoon freshly ground black pepper
- 2 teaspoons dried parsley

Directions:

1. Bring a large pot of water to a boil. Add the cauliflower and garlic. Cook for about 10 minutes or until the cauliflower is fork tender. Drain, return it back to the hot pan, and let it stand for 2 to 3 minutes with the lid on.
2. Transfer the cauliflower and garlic to a food processor or blender. Add the olive oil, salt, and pepper, and purée until smooth.
3. Taste and adjust the salt and pepper. Remove to a serving bowl and add the parsley and mix until combined.
4. Garnish with additional olive oil, if desired. Serve immediately.

Nutrition Info:

- InfoCalories: 87,Total Fat: 4g,Sodium: 210mg,Total Carbohydrate: 12g,Protein: 4.

Brussels Sprouts Casserole

Servings: 6
Cooking Time:x
Ingredients:

- 1 1/2 pounds Brussels sprouts
- 2 thick slices pancetta, diced
- 2 tablespoons chopped shallot
- 2 large cloves garlic, finely minced
- 1/2 cup toasted pine nuts, divided
- 1/2 teaspoon cracked black pepper

Directions:

1. Preheat the oven to 400°F.
2. Bring a large pot of water to a boil. Peel off and discard the outer leaves of the Brussels sprouts and trim the stems. Halve the Brussels sprouts, and add to the boiling water. Boil 10 to 15 minutes, or until the sprouts are easily pierced with a fork. Drain and set aside.
3. Trim the fat from the pancetta before dicing. Heat a large saucepan over medium heat, and add the pancetta. Sauté until brown and crispy, about 4 to 5 minutes. Transfer the pancetta to paper towels to drain. Add the garlic and shallots and half the pine nuts to the same pan. Cook until the nuts turn light brown, about 1 to 2 minutes, and then add the Brussels sprouts. Cook them for an additional 2 to 3 minutes so they absorb the pancetta and garlic flavors. Pour the mixture into an 8- by 8-inch baking dish, season with pepper, and bake for 10 to 15 minutes, or until the tops of the Brussels sprouts brown. Remove from the oven, and top with the remaining pine nuts before serving.

Nutrition Info:

- InfoCalories 128,Total Fat 9 g,Sodium 56 mg,Total Carbohydrate 10 g,Protein 5 .

Whole-grain Crackers

Servings:61
Cooking Time: 10 Minutes

Ingredients:

- 1⁄3 cups white whole-wheat flour
- 1⁄2 teaspoon sodium-free baking powder
- 1 tablespoon all-purpose salt-free seasoning
- 1 teaspoon ground rosemary
- 1 teaspoon garlic powder
- 1⁄2 cup low-fat milk
- 1⁄4 cup grated Parmesan cheese
- 3 tablespoons olive oil
- 1 egg white
- 1–2 tablespoons water, if needed

Directions:

1. Preheat oven to 400°F. Spray a baking sheet lightly with oil and set aside.
2. Place the flour, baking powder, and seasonings into a mixing bowl and whisk well to combine.
3. Add the milk, cheese, olive oil, and egg white and stir to make a stiff dough. Add 1–2 tablespoons of water if the dough is still a little too dry.
4. Turn the dough out onto a lightly floured surface and knead several minutes, until dough is smooth and intact. Roll out to roughly 1⁄8-inch thickness, but no thinner or the crackers will burn. Cut into 1 1⁄2 -inch squares and transfer to the prepared baking sheet.
5. Place baking sheet on middle rack in oven and bake 10 minutes. Remove from oven and place crackers on wire rack to cool. Once cool, store in an airtight container.

Nutrition Info:

- InfoCalories: 95,Fat: 4 g,Protein: 3 g,Sodium: 38 ml,Carbohydrates: 12 .

Southwestern Bean-and-pepper Salad

Servings:4
Cooking Time:x

Ingredients:

- 1 can pinto beans, drained and rinsed
- 2 bell peppers, cored and chopped
- 1 cup corn kernels
- Salt
- Freshly ground black pepper
- Juice of 2 limes
- 1 tablespoon olive oil
- 1 avocado, chopped

Directions:

1. In a large bowl, combine beans, peppers, corn, salt, and pepper. Squeeze fresh lime juice to taste and stir in olive oil. Let the mixture stand in the refrigerator for 30 minutes.
2. Add avocado just before serving.

Nutrition Info:

- InfoCalories: 245,Total Fat: 11g,Sodium: 97mg,Total Carbohydrate: 32g,Protein: 8.

Tart Apple Salad With Fennel And Honey Yogurt Dressing

Servings:6
Cooking Time:x

Ingredients:

- 2 medium green apples, cored and diced
- 1 small bulb fennel, trimmed and chopped
- 1 ½ cups seedless red grape halves
- 2 tablespoons lemon juice
- ¼ cup low-fat vanilla yogurt
- 1 teaspoon honey

Directions:

1. Combine all ingredients in a medium bowl and stir.
2. Serve immediately or cover and refrigerate until ready to serve.

Nutrition Info:

- InfoCalories 70,Fat <1g,Sodium 26mg,Carbohydrates 16g,Protein 1g

Italian Kale And White Beans

Servings:4
Cooking Time:x
Ingredients:

- 1 tablespoon olive oil
- 1 medium yellow onion, chopped
- 3 cloves garlic, minced
- 1 pound dark kale
- ¼ teaspoon kosher salt
- ⅛ teaspoon crushed hot red pepper
- 1 can no-salt-added cannellini beans, drained and rinsed
- 1 tablespoon red wine vinegar

Directions:

1. Heat the oil in a large saucepan over medium heat. Add the onion and garlic and cook, stirring often, until the onion is translucent, about 5 minutes.
2. Meanwhile, pull off and discard the thick stems from the kale. Taking a few pieces at a time, stack the kale and coarsely slice crosswise into ½-inch-thick strips. Transfer to a large bowl of cold water and agitate to loosen any grit. Lift the kale out of the water, leaving behind any dirt. Do not dry the kale.
3. Add the kale, salt, and hot pepper to the saucepan. Cover and cook, stirring occasionally, until the kale is almost tender, about 10 minutes. Stir in the beans and cook, stirring occasionally, until the kale is tender and the beans are heated through, about 5 minutes. Remove from the heat and stir in the vinegar. Serve hot.

Nutrition Info:

- Info233 calories,13 g protein,39 g carbohydrates,5 g fat,180 mg sodiu.

Guacamole With No-salt Corn Chips

Servings:6
Cooking Time: 2 Minutes
Ingredients:

- Tortilla Chips
- Cooking spray
- 4 corn tortillas, cut into triangles
- Guacamole
- 2 avocados, cut into ½-inch cubes
- 1 tablespoon lemon or lime juice
- ¼ cup chopped tomato
- ¼ cup chopped onion
- ¼ cup chopped cilantro
- ¼ cup peeled, seeded, and chopped cucumber

Directions:

1. To make the tortilla chips, preheat oven or toaster oven to 325°F. Spray a small baking sheet or toaster tray with cooking spray. Place tortilla pieces on the baking sheet. Spritz tortilla pieces with cooking spray; bake 2 minutes, or until crisp.
2. To make guacamole, combine avocado and citrus juice in a medium bowl. Mash to blend. Add tomato, onion, cilantro, and cucumber and stir well.
3. Serve guacamole with chips.

Nutrition Info:

- InfoCalories: 96,Fat: 8 g,Sodium: 8 ml,Carbs: 28 g,Protein: 2 .

Arugula With Pears And Red Wine Vinaigrette

Servings:4
Cooking Time:x
Ingredients:

- 8 cups fresh baby arugula
- 2 medium pears, cored and thinly sliced
- ¼ cup chopped pecans
- 4 tablespoons red wine vinegar
- 2 tablespoons olive oil
- 1 clove garlic, peeled and minced
- ½ teaspoon dried marjoram
- ¼ teaspoon ground mustard
- ¼ teaspoon ground black pepper

Directions:

1. Place arugula, pears, and pecans in a large bowl.
2. In a small bowl, whisk together vinegar, oil, garlic, marjoram, mustard, and pepper. Pour over salad and toss to coat. Serve immediately.

Nutrition Info:

- InfoCalories 137,Fat 9g,Sodium 13mg,Carbohydrates 15g,Protein 2g

Broccoli Ziti

Servings:6
Cooking Time:x
Ingredients:

- 1 tablespoon olive oil
- 1 clove garlic, minced
- 1 broccoli head
- 1½ cups ziti or other tubular pasta
- Pinch of kosher salt
- Pinch of freshly ground black pepper

Directions:

1. Bring a large pot of water to a boil over high heat.
2. Heat the oil and garlic together in a small skillet over medium heat, stirring often, until the garlic is softened and fragrant, but not browned, about 2 minutes. Remove from the heat and set aside.
3. Trim the broccoli, cutting the florets from the stalks. Peel the stalks with a vegetable peeler (don't worry about getting every bit of the peel off) and cut crosswise into ¼-inch-thick slices. Cut the florets into bite-sized pieces.
4. Add the broccoli to the boiling water and cook until crisp-tender, about 5 minutes. Using a wire sieve or a skimmer, transfer the broccoli to a bowl. Leave the water boiling.
5. Add the ziti and cook according to the package directions until al dente. During the last minute, return the broccoli to the water. Drain the ziti and broccoli and transfer to a serving bowl. Stir in the garlic-oil mixture, salt, and pepper. Serve hot.

Nutrition Info:

- Info122 calories,5 g protein,20 g carbohydrates,3 g fat,56 mg sodiu.

Homemade Soft Pretzels

Servings:10
Cooking Time:x
Ingredients:

- 4 ½ teaspoons dry active yeast
- 1 ½ cups warm water
- 2 tablespoons honey
- 3 cups unbleached all-purpose flour
- 1 cup white whole-wheat flour
- 1 large egg, beaten

Directions:

1. Preheat oven to 425°F.
2. Place yeast in a large bowl. Add water, honey, and flours and stir to combine. Turn dough out onto a lightly floured surface and knead 5 minutes.
3. Divide dough into 10 equal pieces. Roll each piece into a long snake-like tube, then twist to form a pretzel. Place pretzels on a large baking sheet and brush lightly with the beaten egg.
4. Place baking sheet on middle rack in oven and bake 15 minutes until golden brown. Remove from oven and place pretzels on a wire rack to cool.

Nutrition Info:

- InfoCalories 200,Fat 1g,Sodium 8mg,Carbohydrates 4g,Protein 6g

Maple Mocha Frappe

Servings:2
Cooking Time: 0 Minutes
Ingredients:

- 1 small ripe banana
- 1⁄2 cup brewed coffee
- 1⁄2 cup low-fat milk
- 1 cup low-fat vanilla yogurt
- 1 tablespoon unsweetened cocoa powder
- 2 tablespoons pure maple syrup

Directions:

1. Place the banana in a blender or food processor and purée.
2. Add the remaining ingredients and pulse until smooth and creamy.
3. Serve immediately.

Nutrition Info:

- InfoCalories: 206,Fat: 2 g,Protein: 6 g,Sodium: 116 ml,Carbohydrates: 38 .

Simple Autumn Salad

Servings:4
Cooking Time:x
Ingredients:

- 1 large head red leaf lettuce, torn into bite-sized pieces
- 1 medium pear, cored and thinly sliced
- ½ small red onion, peeled and thinly sliced
- ½ cup chopped dried figs
- ⅓ cup chopped walnuts
- 2 tablespoons white balsamic vinegar
- 2 tablespoons olive oil
- 1 clove garlic, peeled and minced
- ¼ teaspoon ground black pepper

Directions:

1. Place lettuce, pear, onion, figs, and walnuts in a large bowl.
2. In a small bowl, whisk together vinegar, oil, garlic, and pepper. Pour dressing over salad and toss to coat. Serve immediately.

Nutrition Info:

- InfoCalories 224,Fat 14g,Sodium 29mg,Carbohydrates 25g,Protein 3g

Stuffed Sweet Potatoes With Pistachios And Asparagus

Servings:2
Cooking Time:20 Minutes
Ingredients:

- 2 small sweet potatoes, skin well scrubbed
- ½ cup unsalted pistachios
- 2 teaspoons grated Parmesan cheese
- Juice of ½ lemon
- 1 teaspoon reduced-sodium tamari or soy sauce
- 2 teaspoons extra-virgin olive oil
- 2 cloves garlic, minced
- 10 ounces asparagus, tough ends trimmed, chopped
- 2 tablespoons chopped dry-packed sun-dried tomatoes
- Salt and freshly ground black pepper (optional)
- 2 sprigs fresh thyme

Directions:

1. Prick the sweet potatoes all over with a fork. Place on a microwave-safe plate (see Tip) and microwave on high until very tender, 7 to 12 minutes (depending on the size of the sweet potatoes and the power of your microwave). Remove to 2 plates and let cool for 5 minutes. When cool, split the potatoes lengthwise. Being careful of the steam that will release, open the potatoes wide, and mash the flesh with a fork.
2. In a mini food processor, combine the pistachios, Parmesan, lemon juice, and tamari and process until the mixture is sticky and the pistachios are fine.
3. In a medium skillet, heat the olive oil over medium heat. Add the garlic and cook for 1 minute. Add the asparagus and continue cooking until softened, 3 to 5 minutes.
4. Add the pistachio mixture to the asparagus and combine well. Stir in the sun-dried tomatoes and cook for 2 to 3 minutes to soften the tomatoes. Season with salt and pepper, if desired.
5. Scoop half of the mixture into each sweet potato and garnish with fresh thyme.

Nutrition Info:

- InfoCalories 409,Sodium 162 mg,Total carbohydrates 52 g,Protein 13 .

Vegan Caesar Salad Dressing

Servings:1
Cooking Time:x
Ingredients:

- ¼ cup pine nuts or chopped walnuts
- ¼ cup low-sodium vegetable broth
- 2 cloves garlic, peeled
- 1 tablespoon lemon juice
- ¼ teaspoon ground mustard
- ⅛ teaspoon ground white pepper

Directions:

1. Place all ingredients in a food processor and pulse until smooth.
2. Serve immediately.

Nutrition Info:

- InfoCalories 106,Fat 10g,Sodium 10mg,Carbohydrates 4g,Protein 3g

Apple Honey Mustard Vinaigrette

Servings:1
Cooking Time:x
Ingredients:

- ¼ cup apple cider vinegar
- 2 tablespoons honey
- 1 tablespoon olive oil
- 1 teaspoon ground mustard
- ⅛ teaspoon ground white pepper

Directions:

1. Place all ingredients in a small bowl and whisk to combine.
2. Use immediately or cover and refrigerate until ready to serve.

Nutrition Info:

- InfoCalories 65,Fat 3g,Sodium 1mg,Carbohydrates 9g,Protein 0g

Stir-fried Cabbage And Noodles

Servings:6
Cooking Time: 10 Minutes
Ingredients:

- 8 ounces yolkless wide egg noodles
- 1 tablespoon olive oil
- 1/2 medium head green cabbage, chopped
- 1 medium onion, chopped
- 1 teaspoon caraway seeds
- All-purpose salt-free seasoning, to taste
- Freshly ground black pepper, to taste

Directions:

1. Prepare noodles according to package directions, omitting salt. Drain and set aside.
2. Heat olive oil in a large sauté pan over medium heat. Add cabbage and onion and sauté for 5–8 minutes, until tender crisp.
3. Stir in prepared noodles, caraway seeds, salt-free seasoning and freshly ground black pepper, to taste.
4. Serve immediately.

Nutrition Info:

- InfoCalories: 138,Fat: 3 g,Protein: 4 g,Sodium: 22 ml,Carbohydrates: 23 .

Crunchy Coated Nuts

Servings:8
Cooking Time:x
Ingredients:

- 1 egg white
- 3 tablespoons brown sugar
- 2 teaspoons dried oregano
- 3/4 teaspoon ground coriander
- 1/2 teaspoon ground cumin
- 1/4 teaspoon ground cayenne pepper
- Small pinch ground cloves
- 2 cups unsalted mixed nuts

Directions:

1. Preheat oven to 300°F. Line a sided baking sheet with parchment or aluminum foil.
2. Place the egg white and seasonings in a small mixing bowl and whisk until well combined.
3. Add the mixed nuts and toss until evenly coated.
4. Arrange the nuts in a single layer on the baking sheet.
5. Place the baking sheet on the middle rack in the oven and bake 30 minutes, removing the pan halfway through baking time, stirring well, and returning to oven.
6. Remove baking sheet from oven and set on wire rack to cool. Nuts will crisp as they dry and cool, so let them cool fully before removing from the sheet. Store in an airtight container for up to 5 days.

Nutrition Info:

- InfoCalories: 226,Fat: 17 g,Protein: 6 g,Sodium: 13 mg,Carbohydrates: 14 .

Black Bean And Apple Salsa

Servings: 6
Cooking Time:x
Ingredients:

- 1 can black beans, rinsed and drained
- 1/2 large Granny Smith apple, cubed
- 1/4 cup finely chopped red onion
- 1/2 medium serrano chile pepper, unseeded and finely chopped
- 3 tablespoons chopped fresh cilantro
- Juice of 1/2 large lime
- Juice of 1/2 large orange
- 1/8 teaspoon cracked black pepper
- 1/8 teaspoon sea salt

Directions:

1. Combine all the ingredients in a large bowl. Before serving, refrigerate for at least 20 minutes so that the flavors blend.
2. Serving Suggestion: Serve atop a chicken breast, or as a snack or appetizer with unsalted, baked tortilla chips.

Nutrition Info:

- InfoCalories 100,Total Fat 0.4 g,Sodium 50 g,Total Carbohydrate 20 g,Protein 5 .

Beef, Pork, And Lamb

Parmesan Crusted Pork

Servings: 4
Cooking Time: 50 Mins
Ingredients:

- ¼ cup cornflakes, ground to breadcrumb size
- ¼ cup parmesan cheese, finely grated
- 1 tsp fresh thyme, finely chopped
- 2 tsp finely chopped garlic
- Black pepper to taste
- 16-ounce pork tenderloin
- Olive oil in a spray bottle
- 1 small red onion, sliced into thin rounds
- 4 sprigs fresh thyme to garnish

Directions:

1. Make your crumb mixture by mixing the cornflakes, parmesan, thyme, garlic, and black pepper in a shallow dish.
2. Roll the tenderloin in the crumbs, coating thickly and evenly on all sides.
3. Preheat the oven to 375ºF.
4. Lightly oil a baking tray with olive oil, then lay the onion down on the tray. Place the crumbed tenderloin on top of the onions and bake in the oven for about 45-50 minutes.
5. Remove from the oven and then allow the tenderloin to rest for 10 minutes, covered.
6. Slice, and serve hot, garnished with a sprig of thyme.

Nutrition Info:

- Info196 calories,6g carbs,28g protein,316mg sodium,6g fat.

Pressure Cooker Beef Bourguignon

Servings:6
Cooking Time:x
Ingredients:

- 2 tablespoons unsalted butter
- 3 large onions, sliced
- 2 pounds lean beef stew meat, cubed
- 2 cups water
- 1 1⁄2 cups red wine
- 2 teaspoons sodium-free beef bouillon granules
- 1⁄2 teaspoon dried marjoram
- 1⁄2 teaspoon dried thyme
- 1⁄2 teaspoon freshly ground black pepper
- 1 pound white mushrooms, sliced thickly

Directions:

1. Melt the butter in a pressure cooker over medium-high heat. Add the onions and cook, stirring, for 5 minutes.
2. Move onions to the side of the pan, add the cubed beef, and brown on all sides, about 5 minutes.
3. Add the remaining ingredients and stir to combine. Secure the lid on the pressure cooker and set to high. Raise the heat to high and bring contents to a boil. Once you hear sizzling, reduce heat to medium and cook for 20 minutes.
4. Remove from heat. Allow pressure cooker to depressurize naturally, or place under cold running water for about 5 minutes. Serve immediately.

Nutrition Info:

- InfoCalories: 401,Fat: 19 g,Protein: 34 g,Sodium: 115 mg,Carbohydrates: 12 .

Pork Chops With Sweet-and-sour Cabbage

Servings:4
Cooking Time:x

Ingredients:

- Red Cabbage
- 1 slice reduced-sodium bacon, coarsely chopped
- 1 teaspoon canola oil
- 1 medium yellow onion, chopped
- 1 small red cabbage, cored and thinly sliced
- ¼ cup cider vinegar
- 2 Granny Smith apples, cored and cut into ½-inch dice
- ¼ cup water
- 3 tablespoons grade B maple syrup (see "Maple Syrup," here)
- ¼ teaspoon kosher salt
- ¼ teaspoon freshly ground black pepper
- Pork Chops
- Canola oil in a pump sprayer
- 4 boneless center-cut pork chops, excess fat trimmed
- ¼ teaspoon kosher salt
- ¼ teaspoon freshly ground black pepper

Directions:

1. To prepare the red cabbage: In a medium saucepan over medium heat, cook the bacon in the oil, stirring occasionally, until the bacon is crisp and brown, about 5 minutes. Add the onion and cook, stirring occasionally, until golden, about 5 minutes. In three or four additions, stir in the cabbage, sprinkling each addition with a tablespoon or so of the vinegar. Stir in the apples, water, maple syrup, salt, and pepper. Reduce the heat to medium-low and cover tightly. Cook, stirring occasionally, until the cabbage is very tender, about 1 hour. If the liquid cooks away, add a couple of tablespoons of water.
2. To prepare the pork: Spray a large nonstick skillet with oil and heat over medium heat. Season the pork with the salt and pepper and add to the skillet. Cook until the undersides are golden brown, about 3 minutes. Flip the pork and cook until the other sides are golden brown and the meat feels firm when pressed in the thickest part with a fingertip, about 3 minutes more. Transfer to a plate and tent with foil to keep warm.
3. Increase the heat under the skillet to high. Add the red cabbage mixture and any liquid to the skillet and cook, scraping up the browned bits in the skillet with a wooden spoon. Cook until the juices are thickened, about 3 minutes. Return the pork and any juices on the plate to the skillet. Serve hot.

Nutrition Info:

- Info356 calories,29 g protein,39 g carbohydrates,10 g fat,377 mg sodium,1 fa.

Dirty Rice

Servings:4
Cooking Time:x

Ingredients:

- 1/2 pound extra-lean ground beef
- 1 large onion, diced
- 2 medium stalks celery, diced
- 2 cloves garlic, minced
- 1 medium bell pepper, diced
- 1 teaspoon sodium-free beef bouillon granules
- 1 cup water
- 2 teaspoons low-sodium Worcestershire sauce
- 1 1/2 teaspoons dried thyme
- 1 teaspoon dried basil
- 1/2 teaspoon dried marjoram
- 1/4 teaspoon freshly ground black pepper
- Pinch ground cayenne pepper
- 2 scallions, sliced
- 3 cups cooked long-grain brown rice

Directions:

1. Place the ground beef, onion, celery, and garlic into a sauté pan over medium heat. Cook until the beef is browned, roughly 3–5 minutes.
2. Add bell pepper, beef bouillon, water, Worcestershire sauce, and herbs and stir to combine.
3. Bring to a boil, then reduce heat to low, cover, and simmer for 20 minutes.
4. Stir in the scallions and simmer, uncovered, for 3 minutes.
5. Remove from heat. Add the cooked rice and stir well to combine. Serve immediately.

Nutrition Info:

- InfoCalories: 272,Fat: 4 g,Protein: 16 g,Sodium: 92 mg,Carbohydrates: 41 .

Spiced Roast Eye Of Round

Servings:12
Cooking Time:x
Ingredients:

- 1 teaspoon cumin seeds
- 1 teaspoon coriander seeds
- ½ teaspoon whole black peppercorns
- ½ teaspoon kosher salt
- ½ teaspoon ground ginger
- ¼ teaspoon freshly ground black pepper
- ⅛ teaspoon cayenne pepper
- 1 beef eye of round roast, tied
- 1 clove garlic, cut into about 12 slivers
- Olive oil in a pump sprayer

Directions:

1. Position a rack in the center of the oven, and preheat the oven to 400°F.
2. Coarsely crush together the cumin, coriander, and peppercorns in a mortar, in an electric spice grinder, or on a work counter under a heavy skillet. Transfer to a bowl and add the salt, ginger, pepper, and cayenne.
3. Using the tip of a small knife, make 1-inch-deep incisions in the beef and stuff a garlic clove sliver into each slit. Spray the beef with oil and sprinkle with the spice mixture. Place the roast on a meat rack in a roasting pan.
4. Roast for 10 minutes. Reduce the oven temperature to 350°F and continue roasting until an instant-read thermometer inserted in the center of the beef reads 125°F for medium-rare, about 1 hour. Transfer the beef to a carving board and let stand for 10 minutes.
5. Remove the string and cut the meat crosswise into thin slices. Transfer to a serving platter and pour the carving juices over the beef. Serve immediately.

Nutrition Info:

- Info185 calories,33 g protein,0 g carbohydrates,5 g fat,125 mg sodiu.

Beef-and-bean Chili

Servings:4
Cooking Time: 20 Minutes
Ingredients:

- 1 pound lean or extra-lean ground beef
- 1 yellow onion, diced
- 3 cans no-salt diced tomatoes with green chilies (Ro-Tel brand)
- 2 cans beans, drained and rinsed (whatever you desire: black, red, pinto, kidney, etc.)
- 2 tablespoons chili powder
- Optional: 1 package frozen spinach

Directions:

1. In a large stockpot, cook the beef over medium-high heat until browned, stirring frequently. Using a slotted spoon, transfer the cooked beef to a separate plate and set aside. Reserve 1 tablespoon of grease in the stockpot and discard the rest.
2. Add the onion to the stockpot and sauté for 4 to 5 minutes until soft.
3. Add the tomatoes with green chilies, beans, chili powder, and cooked beef to the stockpot, and stir to combine. Bring to a boil, reduce heat to medium-low. Cover and simmer for 10 minutes.
4. Serve immediately.

Nutrition Info:

- InfoCalories: 429,Total Fat: 10g,Sodium: 322mg,Total Carbohydrate: 47g,Protein: 38.

Chinese-style Beef Stir-fry

Servings: 2
Cooking Time: 12 Mins
Ingredients:

- 8 ounces beef sirloin, sliced into strips
- 2 tsp canola oil
- ¾ cup orange juice
- 1 tsp brown sugar
- 1 tbsp. apple cider vinegar
- 1 tsp peanut oil
- 1 tbsp. low sodium soy sauce
- 2 tbsp. corn flour
- ¼ tsp Chines 5-spice mix
- 1 tsp chili flakes
- 3 cups mixed veg, cut stir fry style, frozen
- 2 tsp minced fresh ginger
- 3 tsp finely chopped garlic

Directions:

1. In a pan or a wok, fry the beef off in 1 tsp of hot oil. Fry for about 3-4 minutes, and set aside, covered to stay warm.
2. Make the sauce by combining the orange juice, sugar, vinegar, peanut oil, soy sauce, Chinese 5-spice, chili, and corn flour. Whisk well to incorporate the flour without any lumps.
3. Add the remaining oil to the wok and fry the garlic and ginger off for 1 minute. Add the veg mix and cook until thawed. Add in the sauce and cook for 2 minutes. Lastly, add the beef and cook until heated through and the sauce is thick and shiny.
4. Serve hot. Yum.

Nutrition Info:

- Info321 calories,22g carbs,28g protein,376mg sodium,3g fat.

Beef With Bok Choy

Servings:4
Cooking Time:x
Ingredients:

- 2 pounds bok choy
- 2 teaspoons sesame oil
- 3 cloves garlic, minced
- 1 tablespoon minced fresh ginger
- 1 small red onion, sliced thinly
- 1 teaspoon sodium-free beef bouillon granules
- 1/2 teaspoon ground white pepper
- 1/2 cup water
- 1/2 pound grilled steak, cut into thin slices

Directions:

1. To prepare the bok choy, break the individual stalks off at the base, discarding the small central core. Wash the stalks and greens well, then pat dry. Trim each stalk at the base, then cut the stalks and greens into 2-inch pieces.
2. Heat the oil in a wok over medium heat. Add the garlic, ginger, and onion and cook, stirring, for 30 seconds.
3. Add the bok choy and stir-fry for 2 minutes. Add the bouillon, pepper, and water, raise the heat to high, and cook, stirring, for 5–6 minutes.
4. Add the steak and heat through. Remove from heat and serve immediately.

Nutrition Info:

- InfoCalories: 195,Fat: 10 g,Protein: 20 g,Sodium: 132 mg,Carbohydrates: 5 .

Whole-grain Rotini With Pork, Pumpkin, And Sage

Servings:6
Cooking Time:x

Ingredients:

- 1 package whole-grain rotini
- 1 pound lean ground pork
- 1 medium red onion, diced
- 3 cloves garlic, minced
- 1 medium bell pepper, diced
- 1 cup pumpkin purée
- 2 teaspoons ground sage
- 1 teaspoon ground rosemary
- 1/2–1 teaspoon freshly ground black pepper, to taste

Directions:

1. Cook pasta according to package directions, omitting salt. Drain and set aside.
2. Heat sauté pan over medium heat. Add ground pork, onion, and garlic and sauté for 2 minutes.
3. Add bell pepper and sauté for 5 minutes.
4. Remove from heat. Add pasta to pan along with remaining ingredients. Stir well to combine. Serve immediately.

Nutrition Info:

- InfoCalories: 331,Fat: 7 g,Protein: 23 g,Sodium: 48 mg,Carbohydrates: 45 .

Mini Shepherd's Pies

Servings:4
Cooking Time:x

Ingredients:

- 3 cups diced potato
- 1/2 pound lean ground lamb
- 1 small onion, diced
- 3 cloves garlic, minced
- 1 medium carrot, diced
- 1 medium stalk celery, diced
- 1 cup frozen peas
- 2 tablespoons no-salt-added tomato paste
- 1 teaspoon dried oregano
- 1/2 teaspoon dried basil
- 1/2 teaspoon dried thyme
- 1/4 teaspoon freshly ground black pepper
- 5 tablespoons low-fat milk
- 2 tablespoons nonfat sour cream
- 1 tablespoon unsalted butter
- 1 teaspoon all-purpose salt-free seasoning
- 1 teaspoon onion powder
- 1/2 teaspoon garlic powder
- Freshly ground black pepper, to taste

Directions:

1. Preheat oven to 450°F. Take out 4 ramekins and set aside.
2. Place diced potato in a saucepan and add enough water to cover by 1 inch. Bring to a boil over high heat, then reduce heat to medium and continue boiling for 10 minutes.
3. While the potatoes are boiling, heat a large skillet over medium-high heat. Add lamb, onion, garlic, carrot, and celery and cook, stirring, for 5 minutes.
4. In the last minute of cooking, stir in the peas, tomato paste, and herbs. Spoon contents into the ramekins.
5. Once the potatoes are tender, drain, then mash. Add the remaining ingredients and stir well to combine.
6. Spoon 1/4 of the mashed potato mixture into each ramekin and smooth, making sure edges are completely sealed. Place ramekins on a baking sheet. Place sheet on middle rack in oven and bake for 10 minutes.
7. Remove from oven and serve immediately.

Nutrition Info:

- InfoCalories: 294,Fat: 13 g,Protein: 15 g,Sodium: 89 mg,Carbohydrates: 30 .

Asian-inspired Mini Meatloaves With Salt-free Hoisin Glaze

Servings:4
Cooking Time:x
Ingredients:
- 1⁄2 pound lean ground pork
- 1 medium red bell pepper, diced
- 3⁄4 cup shelled edamame
- 3 scallions, sliced
- 3 cloves garlic, minced
- 1 tablespoon minced fresh ginger
- 1 egg white
- 1⁄3 cup salt-free bread crumbs
- 1⁄2 teaspoon ground 5-spice powder
- 1⁄4 teaspoon ground white pepper
- 3 tablespoons Faux Soy Sauce, divided
- 1 tablespoon salt-free tomato paste

Directions:
1. Preheat oven to 375°F. Spray 4 cups of a jumbo muffin tin lightly with oil and set aside.
2. Place the pork, bell pepper, edamame, scallions, garlic, ginger, egg white, bread crumbs, 5-spice powder, and pepper into a bowl. Add 1 tablespoon Faux Soy Sauce and mix together using your (freshly washed) hands.
3. Divide mixture into 4 equal portions and press into the prepared muffin tin.
4. Measure the remaining 2 tablespoons Faux Soy Sauce and tomato paste into a small bowl and stir until smooth. Brush onto the tops of the meatloaves, dividing evenly.
5. Place muffin tin on middle rack in oven and bake for 30 minutes.
6. Remove from oven, gently run a knife around the sides of each loaf, and remove from tin. Serve immediately.
Nutrition Info:
- InfoCalories: 205,Fat: 6 g,Protein: 17 g,Sodium: 56 mg,Carbohydrates: 20 .

Basil Pesto

Servings:1
Cooking Time: 0 Minutes
Ingredients:
- 2 cups fresh basil leaves
- 4 cloves garlic
- 3 tablespoons olive oil
- 1⁄4 cup walnuts, almonds, or pine nuts
- 2 tablespoons grated Parmesan cheese
- 1⁄4 teaspoon freshly ground black pepper

Directions:
1. Place all the ingredients into a food processor and pulse until smooth.
2. Use immediately or store in an airtight container and refrigerate until use.
Nutrition Info:
- InfoCalories: 166,Fat: 17 g,Protein: 2 g,Sodium: 39 ml,Carbohydrates: 2 .

Spicy Sichuan Orange Beef Vegetable Stir-fry

Servings:2
Cooking Time:12 Minutes
Ingredients:
- ¾ cup orange juice
- 1 tablespoon reduced-sodium soy sauce (see Tip)
- 1 tablespoon unseasoned rice vinegar or dry sherry
- 1 teaspoon sesame oil
- 2 teaspoons cornstarch
- ¼ teaspoon Chinese five-spice powder
- 1 teaspoon red pepper flakes
- 2 teaspoons extra-virgin olive oil
- 8 ounces boneless beef sirloin steak, cut into thin strips
- 3 cloves garlic, minced
- 2 teaspoons grated fresh ginger
- 3 cups frozen stir-fry vegetable blend

Directions:
1. In a small bowl, combine the orange juice, soy sauce, rice vinegar, sesame oil, cornstarch, five-spice, and pepper flakes until smooth. Set aside.
2. In a large skillet or wok, heat 1 teaspoon of the olive oil over high heat. Add the beef and stir-fry until no longer pink, 3 to 4 minutes. Remove with a slotted spoon to a plate; cover to keep warm.
3. Add the remaining 1 teaspoon olive oil to the pan. Add the garlic and ginger and stir-fry for 1 minute. Add the vegetables and continue cooking for 2 to 3 minutes, until thawed. Stir the sauce and pour into the pan, bring to a boil, and cook for 2 to 3 minutes to thicken. Return the beef to the pan, stir to combine, and cook for an additional 1 to 2 minutes to heat through.

Nutrition Info:
- InfoCalories 321,Sodium 376 mg,Total carbohydrates 22 g,Protein 28 .

Sweet And Savory Apple-cinnamon Baked Pork Chops

Servings:4
Cooking Time:40 Minutes
Ingredients:
- 2 apples, peeled and sliced
- 1 teaspoon ground cinnamon
- 4 boneless pork chops (½ inch thick)
- 1 medium red onion, halved and thinly sliced
- ⅛ teaspoon salt
- Freshly ground black pepper (optional)
- 3 tablespoons dark brown sugar
- 1 tablespoon extra-virgin olive oil

Directions:
1. Preheat the oven to 375° F.
2. Layer the apples in the bottom of a casserole dish. Sprinkle with ½ teaspoon of the cinnamon.
3. Trim the fat from the pork chops. Lay them on top of the apple slices. Layer the pork chops with the onion slices. Sprinkle with the salt and black pepper, if desired.
4. In a small bowl, combine ¾ cup water (see Tip), the brown sugar, and the remaining ½ teaspoon cinnamon. Pour the mixture over the chops. Drizzle with the olive oil.
5. Transfer to the oven and bake, uncovered, until an instant-read thermometer reads 145°F, 30 to 45 minutes. Allow to rest for 3 minutes before serving.

Nutrition Info:
- InfoCalories 325,Sodium 126 mg,Total carbohydrates 24 g,Protein 24 .

Sweet & Sour Pork Chops

Servings: 4
Cooking Time: 70 Mins
Ingredients:

- Sweet and Sour Cabbage:
- 1 tbsp. olive oil
- 1 medium red onion, sliced
- 2 rashers low sodium back bacon, cut into cubes
- ½ medium sized white cabbage, sliced
- ¼ cup white grape vinegar
- 3 tbsp. golden syrup
- ¼ cup water
- 2 crisp green apples, peeled and diced
- Black pepper to taste
- Pork Chops:
- Olive oil in a spray bottle
- 4 4-ounce pork chops, fat removed
- Black pepper to taste

Directions:

1. Heat the oil in a pan, add the onion and fry for 1 minute. Then add the bacon pieces and cook until crispy and browned. Add ⅓ of the cabbage, and sprinkle over ⅓ of the vinegar. Repeat this process until the cabbage and vinegar are all incorporated.
2. Then add the syrup, water, apples, and black pepper and reduce the heat. Leave to simmer on low for about 1 hour.
3. 10 minutes before the cabbage is ready, heat and oil a non-stick pan.
4. Place the pork chops in the pan and fry until golden brown on each side, about 3 minutes a side. While cooking, add black pepper to taste. Set aside covered to keep warm.
5. Transfer the cabbage mixture to the hot chops pan and stir well on high for 3 minutes.
6. To serve, use a slotted spoon. To avoid getting juices on the plate, spoon the cabbage mixture neatly onto the center of the plate and place the hot chops on top.
7. Enjoy.

Nutrition Info:

- Info356 calories,39g carbs,29g protein,377mg sodium,10g fat.

Beef And Bulgur Meat Loaf

Servings:8
Cooking Time:x
Ingredients:

- 1 cup boiling water
- ½ cup bulgur
- 2 teaspoons canola oil, plus more in a pump sprayer
- 1 medium yellow onion, chopped
- 1 medium red bell pepper, cored and cut into ¼-inch dice
- 2 cloves garlic, minced
- ¼ cup plus 2 tablespoons low-salt tomato ketchup
- 1 tablespoon Worcestershire sauce (see note here)
- 1 teaspoon kosher salt
- ½ teaspoon freshly ground black pepper
- 2 large egg whites
- 1 pound ground sirloin

Directions:

1. In a heatproof medium bowl, combine the boiling water and bulgur and let stand until the bulgur has softened and absorbed the water, about 20 minutes.
2. Meanwhile, preheat the oven to 350°F. Line a rimmed baking sheet with aluminum foil and spray with oil.
3. Heat the 2 teaspoons oil in a medium nonstick skillet over medium heat. Add the onion, bell pepper, and garlic and cook, stirring occasionally, until tender, about 6 minutes. Transfer to a bowl and cool slightly.
4. Drain the bulgur in a wire sieve, pressing hard on the bulgur to extract the excess water. Add to the bowl with the vegetables, then stir in ¼ cup of the ketchup, Worcestershire sauce, salt, and pepper. (Adding these ingredients at this point helps to cool the vegetables so the egg whites won't cook from the heat.) Stir in the egg whites. Add the ground sirloin and mix just until combined. Shape into an 8 × 4-inch loaf on the foil-lined baking sheet.
5. Bake until the loaf is golden brown and an instant-read thermometer inserted in the center reads 165°F, about 40 minutes. During the last 5 minutes, spread the top of the loaf with the 2 tablespoons ketchup.
6. Let stand for 10 minutes. Slice and serve hot.

Nutrition Info:

- Info162 calories,15 g protein,16 g carbohydrates,4 g fat,322 mg sodiu.

Beef And Mushrooms With Sour Cream–dill Sauce

Servings:4
Cooking Time:x
Ingredients:

- 2 teaspoons canola oil, plus more in a pump sprayer
- 1 pound sirloin steak, excess fat trimmed, cut across the grain in ½-inch-thick slices and then into 2-inch-wide pieces
- 12 ounces cremini mushrooms, sliced
- ¼ cup finely chopped shallots
- 2 teaspoons cornstarch
- ¾ cup Homemade Beef Stock (here)
- ½ cup reduced-fat sour cream
- 1 tablespoon finely chopped fresh dill
- ½ teaspoon kosher salt
- ½ teaspoon freshly ground black pepper

Directions:

1. Spray a large nonstick skillet with oil and heat over medium-high heat. Add half of the sirloin and cook, flipping the sirloin pieces halfway through cooking, until browned on both sides, about 2 minutes. Transfer to a plate. Repeat with the remaining sirloin.
2. Heat the 2 teaspoons oil in the skillet over medium heat. Add the mushrooms and cook, stirring occasionally, until their liquid evaporates and they begin to brown, about 6 minutes. Stir in the shallots and cook until softened, about 1 minute.
3. In a small bowl, sprinkle the cornstarch over the broth and stir to dissolve. Stir into the mushrooms and cook until boiling and thickened. Stir in the sour cream, dill, salt, and pepper. Return the sirloin and any juices on the plate to the skillet and cook just until heated through, about 30 seconds. Serve hot.

Nutrition Info:

- Info275 calories,31 g protein,9 g carbohydrates,13 g fat,354 mg sodium,1 fat.

Pork Medallions With Spring Succotash

Servings:4
Cooking Time: 20 Minutes
Ingredients:

- 1 pound pork tenderloin, trimmed and cut into 1-inch-thick slices
- 2 teaspoons minced garlic
- 1 teaspoon dried rosemary
- 1½ tablespoons olive oil, divided
- 1 cup low-sodium chicken stock
- 1 cup carrots, halved and thinly sliced
- 3 tablespoons water
- ½ teaspoon freshly ground black pepper
- 2 cups frozen lima beans, thawed
- 1 cup frozen spinach, thawed

Directions:

1. Using a meat mallet or the heel of your hand, gently pound the pork slices until they are ½-inch-thick medallions.
2. In a small bowl, combine the garlic and rosemary.
3. In a large skillet, heat 1 tablespoon of olive oil over medium heat and swirl to coat. Add the pork and cook, without turning, for 4 minutes. Turn and cook for 3 minutes, or until it reaches your desired doneness. Place the pork in a bowl or plate and cover to keep warm.
4. In the same skillet, sauté the garlic mixture for 1 minute, until fragrant. Add the chicken stock and cook for 30 seconds, until reduced to ½ cup. Remove the pan from heat.
5. In another large nonstick skillet, heat the remaining olive oil over medium heat and swirl to coat. Add the carrots and cook for 2 minutes. Stir in the water and pepper. Cover and cook for 2 minutes, until the carrots are crisp and tender. Add the lima beans and spinach, cooking for 3 minutes or until heated through.
6. Divide the vegetable mixture among 4 plates and top each serving with pork and sauce.

Nutrition Info:

- InfoCalories: 317,Total Fat: 11g,Sodium: 150mg,Total Carbohydrate: 28g,Protcin: 28.

Apple-cinnamon Baked Pork Chops

Servings:4
Cooking Time: 40 Minutes
Ingredients:
- 2 apples, peeled, cored, and sliced
- 1 teaspoon ground cinnamon, divided
- 4 boneless pork chops (½-inch thick)
- Salt
- Freshly ground black pepper
- ¾ cup water
- 3 tablespoons brown sugar
- 1 tablespoon olive oil

Directions:
1. Preheat the oven to 375°F. Layer apples in bottom of casserole dish. Sprinkle with ½ teaspoon of cinnamon.
2. Trim fat from the pork chops. Lay chops on top of the apple slices. Sprinkle with a dash of salt and pepper.
3. In a small bowl, combine ¾ cup of water, brown sugar, and remaining cinnamon. Pour the mixture over the chops. Drizzle the chops with 1 tablespoon of olive oil.
4. Bake uncovered in preheated oven for 30 to 45 minutes or until an instant-read thermometer registers between 145°F and 160°F. Allow to rest for 3 minutes before serving.

Nutrition Info:
- InfoCalories: 244,Total Fat: 10g,Sodium: 254mg,Total Carbohydrate: 22g,Protein: 21.

Orange-beef Stir-fry

Servings:2
Cooking Time: 10 Minutes
Ingredients:
- 1 tablespoon cornstarch
- ¼ cup cold water
- ¼ cup orange juice
- 1 tablespoon reduced-sodium soy sauce
- 2 teaspoons olive oil, divided
- ½ pound boneless beef sirloin steak, cut into thin strips
- 3 cups frozen stir-fry vegetable blend
- 1 garlic clove, minced

Directions:
1. In a small bowl, mix the cornstarch, water, orange juice, and soy sauce until smooth. Set the mixture aside.
2. In a large wok or skillet, heat 1 teaspoon of olive oil over medium-high heat. Stir-fry the beef for 3 to 4 minutes, until no longer pink. Remove to a plate or bowl and cover to keep warm.
3. Add the remaining olive oil to the wok and allow to heat. Stir-fry the vegetable blend and garlic for 3 minutes. Stir the cornstarch mixture, then add it to the cooking vegetables and bring to a boil. Stir for 2 minutes, until thickened. Add the beef and stir until heated through.

Nutrition Info:
- InfoCalories: 268,Total Fat: 10g,Sodium: 376mg,Total Carbohydrate: 8g,Protein: 26.

Poultry

Turkey Mini Meat Loaf With Dijon Glaze

Servings:4
Cooking Time:x
Ingredients:

- 2 teaspoons canola oil, plus more in a pump sprayer
- 1 medium yellow onion, finely chopped
- 1 medium carrot, cut into ¼-inch dice
- 1 medium celery stalk, cut into ¼-inch dice
- 1 tablespoon water
- 1¼ pounds ground turkey
- ¾ cup old-fashioned (rolled) oats
- 1 large egg, beaten
- 1 teaspoon dried rosemary
- ½ teaspoon kosher salt
- ¼ teaspoon freshly ground black pepper
- 1 tablespoon Dijon mustard
- 1 tablespoon honey

Directions:

1. Preheat the oven to 350°F. Line a large baking sheet with aluminum foil and spray with oil.
2. Heat the 2 teaspoons oil in a medium nonstick skillet over medium heat. Add the onion, carrot, celery, and water. Cook, stirring occasionally, until the vegetables are tender, about 10 minutes. Transfer to a medium bowl and let cool slightly.
3. Add the ground turkey, oats, egg, rosemary, salt, and pepper and mix gently but thoroughly until combined. Divide into four equal portions and shape each on the prepared baking sheet, about 2 inches apart, into a 5 × 3-inch loaf.
4. Bake until lightly browned and an instant-read thermometer inserted in the center of a loaf reads about 160°F, about 35 minutes. Remove from the oven. Mix the mustard and honey in a small bowl, then spread the top of each loaf with one-quarter of the mustard mixture. Return to the oven and continue baking until the mustard mixture is glazed, about 5 minutes more. Let stand at room temperature for 5 minutes before serving.

Nutrition Info:

- Info335 calories,32 g protein,21 g carbohydrates,15 g fat,484 mg sodium,2 fats.

Turkey Cutlets With Lemon And Basil Sauce

Servings:4
Cooking Time:x
Ingredients:

- 1 pound turkey cutlets, cut into 8 serving pieces
- ½ teaspoon kosher salt
- ¼ teaspoon freshly ground black pepper
- ¼ cup whole-wheat flour
- 4 teaspoons olive oil
- 1 cup Homemade Chicken Broth (here) or canned low-sodium chicken broth
- Grated zest of ½ lemon
- 3 tablespoons fresh lemon juice
- 2 tablespoons dry vermouth
- 1 tablespoon cold unsalted butter
- 2 tablespoons finely chopped fresh basil

Directions:

1. Season the turkey with the salt and pepper. Spread the flour on a plate, and coat the turkey with the flour, shaking off the excess. Heat 2 teaspoons of the oil in a large nonstick skillet over medium heat. Add half of the turkey to the skillet and cook, flipping the turkey halfway through cooking, until lightly browned on both sides, about 4 minutes. Transfer to a plate. Repeat with the remaining 2 teaspoons oil and the turkey, and add to the turkey on the plate.
2. Combine the broth, lemon zest and juice, and vermouth in the skillet and bring to a boil over high heat. Cook until reduced by half, about 5 minutes. Return all of the turkey to the skillet and reduce the heat to medium. Cook, turning the turkey in the sauce, until the sauce is lightly thickened and the turkey is opaque when pierced in the center with the tip of a sharp knife, about 2 minutes. Transfer the turkey to a serving platter.
3. Remove the skillet from the heat. Whisk in the butter, then 1 tablespoon of the basil. Pour over the turkey, and sprinkle with the remaining 1 tablespoon basil. Serve hot.

Nutrition Info:

- Info208 calories,29 g protein,2 g carbohydrates,8 g fat,365 mg sodium,2 fats.

Moo Shu Chicken And Vegetable Wraps

Servings:6
Cooking Time:x
Ingredients:

- Sauce
- ⅓ cup Homemade Chicken Broth (here) or canned low-sodium chicken broth
- 1 tablespoon rice vinegar
- 1 tablespoon no-salt-added tomato ketchup
- 1 tablespoon reduced-sodium soy sauce
- 1 teaspoon Asian sesame oil
- 2 teaspoons cornstarch
- Chicken
- 4 teaspoons canola oil
- 1 boneless, skinless chicken breast half, cut across the grain into ¼-inch-thick bite-sized pieces
- 10 ounces shiitake mushroom caps, sliced
- 1 package broccoli slaw
- 3 scallions, white and green parts, cut into 1-inch lengths
- 1 can sliced water chestnuts, drained and rinsed
- 1 tablespoon peeled and minced fresh ginger
- 2 cloves garlic, minced
- Wraps
- 12 Boston or Bibb lettuce leaves

Directions:
1. To make the sauce: In a small bowl, whisk together the broth, vinegar, ketchup, soy sauce, sesame oil, and cornstarch.
2. To prepare the chicken: Heat 2 teaspoons of the oil in a large nonstick skillet over medium-high heat. Add the chicken and cook, stirring occasionally, until it turns opaque throughout, about 4 minutes. Transfer to a plate.
3. Heat the remaining 2 teaspoons oil in the skillet over medium-high heat. Add the mushrooms and cook, stirring occasionally, until softened, about 5 minutes. Add the broccoli slaw, scallions, and water chestnuts and cook, stirring often, until the slaw is hot and wilted, about 3 minutes. Add the ginger and garlic and cook until fragrant, about 1 minute more. Stir the reserved chicken and sauce mixture and add to the skillet. Stir until the sauce is thickened and boiling, about 30 seconds.
4. To serve, transfer the chicken mixture to a serving bowl. Let each person spoon the chicken mixture onto a lettuce leaf, roll it up, and enjoy.

Nutrition Info:
- Info144 calories,11 g protein,15 g carbohydrates,5 g fat,168 mg sodium,1 fat.

Chicken And Apple Curry

Servings:4
Cooking Time:x
Ingredients:

- 2 teaspoons canola oil, plus more in a pump sprayer
- 2 boneless, skinless chicken breast halves, trimmed, pounded to ¾-inch thickness, and cut into 4 equal serving portions
- 1 medium yellow onion, chopped
- 2 medium celery ribs, chopped
- 2 Granny Smith apples, peeled, cored, and cut into ½-inch dice
- 1 tablespoon curry powder
- ¾ cup light coconut milk
- ½ cup water
- 2 tablespoons fresh lime juice
- ½ cup sliced natural almonds, for serving

Directions:
1. Spray a large nonstick skillet with oil and heat over medium-high heat. Add the chicken and cook, flipping halfway through cooking, until lightly browned on both sides, about 6 minutes. Transfer to a plate.
2. Heat the 2 teaspoons oil in the skillet over medium heat. Add the onion, celery, and apples and cook, stirring often, until the onion is tender, about 5 minutes. Sprinkle in the curry powder and stir well.
3. Stir in the coconut milk, water, and lime juice and bring to a simmer, stirring often. Add the chicken and cover. Reduce the heat to medium-low and simmer until the chicken is opaque when pierced in the center with the tip of a small, sharp knife, about 6 minutes.
4. Transfer the chicken to a deep serving platter. Increase the heat under the skillet to high and boil the sauce until lightly thickened, about 1 minute. Pour the sauce mixture over the chicken and sprinkle with the almonds. Serve hot.

Nutrition Info:
- Info444 calories,35 g protein,26 g carbohydrates,24 g fat,192 mg sodiu.

Turkey And Brown Rice Stuffed Peppers

Servings:4
Cooking Time:x
Ingredients:

- 4 large bell peppers
- 1 pound lean ground turkey
- 1 medium onion, diced
- 3 cloves garlic, minced
- 2 medium stalks celery, diced
- 2 cups cooked brown rice
- 1 can no-salt-added diced tomatoes
- 2 tablespoons salt-free tomato paste
- 1/4 cup seedless raisins
- 2 teaspoons ground cumin
- 1 teaspoon dried oregano
- 1/2 teaspoon ground cinnamon
- 1/2 teaspoon freshly ground black pepper

Directions:

1. Preheat the oven to 425°F. Lightly spray a 9 × 13" baking pan with oil and set aside.
2. Wash and dry the peppers. Trim about 1/2 inch off the top and place caps aside. Carefully core and seed, leaving the peppers intact. Trim bottoms if necessary so that the peppers sit flat. Set aside.
3. Heat a sauté pan over medium heat. Add the ground turkey, onion, garlic, and celery and sauté for 5 minutes. Remove from heat.
4. Stir in the remaining ingredients and mix well.
5. Fill each pepper with 1/4 of the mixture, pressing firmly to pack. Stand peppers in the prepared baking pan, replace the pepper caps, and then cover pan tightly with foil. Place pan on middle rack in oven and bake until tender, about 25–30 minutes.
6. Remove from oven and serve immediately.

Nutrition Info:

- InfoCalories: 354,Fat: 8 g,Protein: 27 g,Sodium: 126 mg,Carbohydrates: 45 .

Seasoned Turkey Burgers With Sautéed Mushrooms And Swiss

Servings:4
Cooking Time:x
Ingredients:

- 1 pound lean ground turkey
- 2 cloves garlic, peeled and minced
- 1 tablespoon no-salt-added prepared mustard
- 2 teaspoons low-sodium Worcestershire sauce
- 1 teaspoon salt-free Italian seasoning
- ½ teaspoon ground black pepper
- 1 teaspoon olive oil
- 3 cups sliced mushrooms
- 4 Soft and Crusty No-Rise Rolls
- ½ cup shredded Swiss cheese

Directions:

1. Place ground turkey in a large bowl. Add garlic, mustard, Worcestershire sauce, Italian seasoning, and pepper and mix using your hands.
2. Divide mixture into 4 equal parts. Roll each portion into a round ball, then flatten and form into patties.
3. Grill or broil the burgers until they reach an internal temperature of 165°F. If grilling, they'll take 5–6 minutes per side; if broiling, they'll take 4–6 minutes per side. Remove burgers from heat, cover, and set aside.
4. Heat oil in a medium skillet over medium heat. Add mushrooms and sauté for 5 minutes. Remove from heat.
5. Sandwich each burger in a bun, dividing sautéed mushrooms and cheese evenly among them. Serve immediately.

Nutrition Info:

- InfoCalories 377,Fat 14g,Sodium 145mg,Carbohydrates 31g,Protein 32g

Turkey-spinach Meatballs With Tomato Sauce

Servings:6
Cooking Time:x
Ingredients:

- Turkey-Spinach Meatballs
- 1 box frozen chopped spinach, thawed and squeezed to remove excess liquid
- 1 medium yellow onion, shredded on the large holes of a box grater
- 2 cloves garlic, minced
- ⅓ cup whole-wheat bread crumbs, made from day-old bread pulsed in the blender
- 2 large egg whites, or ¼ cup seasoned liquid egg substitute
- 1 teaspoon Italian Seasoning (here) or dried oregano
- 1 teaspoon kosher salt
- ½ teaspoon freshly ground black pepper
- 1¼ pounds ground turkey
- Olive oil in a pump sprayer
- ½ cup water
- Tomato Sauce
- 1 tablespoon olive oil
- 1 medium yellow onion, chopped
- 2 cloves garlic, minced
- 1 can no-salt-added crushed tomatoes
- 2 teaspoons Italian Seasoning (here) or dried oregano
- ¼ teaspoon crushed hot red pepper
- 6 tablespoons freshly grated Parmesan cheese (optional)

Directions:

1. To make the meatballs: In a large bowl, mix the spinach, onion, garlic, bread crumbs, egg whites, Italian Seasoning, salt, and pepper. Add the ground turkey and combine thoroughly. Refrigerate for 15 to 30 minutes to firm the mixture and make it easier to handle.
2. Roll the turkey mixture into 18 meatballs. Spray a large nonstick skillet with oil and heat over medium heat. In batches, add the meatballs and cook, turning occasionally, until lightly browned, about 6 minutes. Transfer to a plate. Add the water to the skillet and bring to a boil, stirring up the browned bits in the pan with a wooden spoon. Remove from the heat.
3. To make the sauce: Heat the oil in a medium saucepan over medium heat. Add the onion and sauté, stirring occasionally, until golden and tender, about 5 minutes. Stir in the garlic and cook until fragrant, about 1 minute. Add the liquid from the skillet, the tomatoes, Italian Seasoning, and hot pepper; combine thoroughly and bring to a boil. Reduce the heat to medium-low and simmer, stirring occasionally, until lightly thickened, about 15 minutes. Bury the meatballs in the sauce and cook until the meatballs show no sign of pink when pierced to the center with the tip of a sharp knife, about 15 minutes more. Divide the meatballs and sauce among six bowls, sprinkle each with 1 tablespoon of the Parmesan (if using), and serve hot.

Nutrition Info:

- Info240 calories,22 g protein,16 g carbohydrates,10 g fat,513 mg sodium,1 fat.

Sweet Chili Chicken Wrap

Servings: 4
Cooking Time:x
Ingredients:

- 4 large wholegrain wraps
- 2/3 cup sweet chili mayonnaise mixture, store-bought
- 2 cups cooked pulled chicken breast
- ¼ cup white cabbage, cut chiffonade style
- 2 spring onions, sliced
- ¼ cup grated carrot
- ¼ cucumber, peeled, deseeded, and thinly shaved with a peeler
- 2 tbsp. fresh coriander, chopped
- 2 small avocados, cut into cubes
- Spray bottle of olive oil

Directions:

1. Lightly coat the cooked chicken in ⅓ cup of sweet chili mayonnaise. Then, in a bowl, mix the chicken, cabbage, onion, carrot, cucumber, coriander, and avocado together.
2. Divide the mixture into 4 and roll the wraps, making sure to fold over the ends to prevent the mixture from falling out.
3. Heat a non-stick pan, lightly spray with oil, and then toast the wraps lightly on all sides until golden brown.
4. Cut in half and serve warm with the remaining ⅓cup sweet chili mayonnaise.

Nutrition Info:

- Info228 calories,19g carbs,31g protein,368mg sodium,5g fat.

Spicy Chicken Mac N Cheese

Servings: 4
Cooking Time: 26 Mins
Ingredients:

- 8 ounces macaroni pasta
- 1 tbsp. flour
- 1 tbsp. unsalted butter
- 2 cups low fat milk
- Olive oil in a spray bottle
- ½ cup finely chopped white onion
- ¼ low fat mascarpone cheese
- ¼ tsp garlic powder
- Black pepper to taste
- 2 tbsp. Buffalo hot sauce, plus extra to serve
- 12 ounces cooked pulled chicken breast
- 2 tbsp. feta crumbled feta cheese
- ½ cup grated mature cheddar cheese

Directions:
1. Bring a medium pot of water to a boil. Add the pasta and cook for about 9 minutes, or until al dente. Drain and cover to keep warm.
2. Next, make your white sauce. Melt the butter in a small pot, then add the four and whisk vigorously to prevent lumps from forming. Gradually add the milk, whisking all the time. After 2 minutes, add the mascarpone, garlic powder and pepper and stir for another 3 minutes.
3. Meanwhile, fry off the onion until soft using a little olive oil.
4. Then add the Buffalo sauce, grated cheese, and feta to the sauce. Stir for 1 minute, and lastly, add in the onions.
5. Bring the dish together by adding the pulled chicken and pasta into the sauce and stirring well.
6. Spoon into serving bowls hot and serve with additional buffalo sauce

Nutrition Info:
- Info541 calories,52g carbs,44g protein,537mg sodium,16g fat.

Low-sodium Kung Pao Chicken

Servings:4
Cooking Time:x
Ingredients:

- 1 cup low-sodium chicken broth
- 2 tablespoons Faux Soy Sauce
- 1 tablespoon balsamic vinegar
- 5 tablespoons cornstarch, divided
- 2 teaspoons sesame oil
- 1 teaspoon sugar
- 1 pound boneless, skinless chicken breasts, cubed
- 1/4 teaspoon freshly ground black pepper
- 2 tablespoons canola oil, divided
- 1/4 teaspoon dried red pepper flakes
- 2 tablespoons minced fresh ginger
- 6 scallions, sliced, whites and greens kept separate
- 1 medium red bell pepper, cubed
- 2 medium stalks celery, sliced
- 2 medium carrots, sliced
- 1/4 cup plain unflavored rice vinegar
- 1/4 cup unsalted cashews or peanuts, chopped

Directions:
1. Place the chicken broth, Faux Soy Sauce, balsamic vinegar, 1 tablespoon cornstarch, sesame oil, and sugar into a bowl. Whisk well to combine and set aside.
2. Place the chicken into a mixing bowl, add 4 tablespoons cornstarch and black pepper, to taste, and toss well to coat using a pair of tongs.
3. Heat 1 tablespoon oil in a sauté pan over medium heat. Add the chicken and cook until lightly browned on all sides, about 4 minutes total.
4. Add the remaining tablespoon oil to the pan. Add the red pepper flakes, ginger, and whites of the scallions and cook, stirring, for 1 minute.
5. Add the bell pepper, celery, and carrots and sauté until they soften slightly, about 2 minutes.
6. Add the rice vinegar and scrape the bottom of the pan to incorporate any browned bits.
7. Give the chicken broth mixture a quick whisk, then add to the pan.
8. Check the chicken. If still pink inside, reduce heat and cook a couple minutes more. Remove pan from heat and serve immediately, sprinkled with the chopped nuts and scallion greens.

Nutrition Info:
- InfoCalories: 347,Fat: 14 g,Protein: 29 g,Sodium: 135 mg,Carbohydrates: 24 .

Nut-crusted Chicken

Servings: 4
Cooking Time: 25 Mins
Ingredients:

- 4 4-ounce chicken breasts, deboned and skin removed
- 1 tbsp. olive oil
- 1 tsp ground cayenne pepper
- ½ tsp ground black pepper
- ½ cup pecan nuts
- ½ cup flax seeds, ground into meal
- 4 cups green beans, topped and tailed and cut in half
- 1 lemon, cut into quarters

Directions:

1. Lightly oil a baking tray using an oil brush.
2. Preheat the oven to 350ºF and then blitz the nuts in a blender to form a meal.
3. Mix the ground nuts, flax meal, cayenne pepper, and black pepper. Then put this mixture into a bag. It can be a resealable plastic one or a brown paper bag.
4. Add the chicken breasts to the bag, make sure it is well sealed at the top and give it a good shake. Make sure to coat all the sides of the chicken with the crust mixture.
5. Place the crusted chicken pieces on the baking tray and bake for about 25-30 minutes or until a food thermometer reads 165 ºF at the center of the chicken. Discard the remaining crust mixture.
6. Bring a small pot of water to a boil.
7. 5 minutes before the chicken is cooked, blanch the green beans in boiling water, cooking them until still crunchy and bright green. Drain off the water.
8. Serve the chicken hot alongside the beans and finish it off with a lemon quarter.

Nutrition Info:

- Info310 calories,14g carbs,31g protein,308mg sodium,18g fat.

Mexican Chicken Breast With Tomatillo Salsa

Servings:4
Cooking Time:x
Ingredients:

- Tomatillo Sauce
- 8 ounces tomatillos (preferably all the same size), husked
- 2 scallions, white and green parts, coarsely chopped
- ½ jalapeño, seeded and minced
- 1 tablespoon fresh lime juice
- 1 tablespoon coarsely chopped fresh cilantro
- 1 clove garlic, crushed under a knife and peeled
- Pinch of kosher salt
- Chicken
- Olive oil in a pump sprayer
- 2 boneless, skinless chicken breast halves, pounded to ¾-inch thickness and cut in half to make 4 portions
- 1 tablespoon Mexican Seasoning (here)
- Lime wedges, for serving

Directions:

1. To make the sauce: Bring a medium saucepan of water to a boil over high heat. Add the tomatillos and reduce the heat to medium. Cook at a moderate boil just until they turn olive green, using a slotted spoon to transfer the tomatillos from the water to a bowl as they are ready, about 5 minutes. Do not overcook or the tomatillos will burst. Carefully drain the tomatillos.
2. In a food processor (or a blender with its lid ajar), puree the drained tomatillos, scallions, jalapeño, lime juice, cilantro, garlic, and salt. Set aside.
3. To prepare the chicken: Spray a large nonstick skillet with oil and heat over medium heat. Spray the chicken on both sides with the oil and sprinkle with the Mexican Seasoning. Add the chicken to the skillet and cook, turning halfway through cooking, until golden brown on both sides, about 6 minutes.
4. Pour in the tomatillo salsa and simmer until the chicken is opaque when pierced in the thickest part with the tip of a sharp knife, 6 to 8 minutes. Serve hot with the lime wedges.

Nutrition Info:

- Info190 calories,31 g protein,6 g carbohydrates,4 g fat,208 mg sodiu.

Louisiana Turkey Burgers

Servings: 4
Cooking Time: 17 Mins
Ingredients:

- ½ cup apple cider vinegar
- 1 small red onion, thinly sliced
- 2 tsp olive oil, plus extra in a spray bottle
- 20-ounces turkey mince
- 2 small shallots, diced
- 1 small sweet paprika pepper, cut into cubes
- 2 tsp minced fresh garlic
- 4 tbsp. finely chopped fresh parsley
- 1 stalk celery, diced
- 1 tsp readymade Cajun spice mix
- 4 whole Ciabatta burger buns
- ¼ cup low fat mayonnaise
- 1 tsp Dijon mustard
- 1 cup rocket leaves
- 4 slices Roma tomato

Directions:
1. Cover the sliced red onion in vinegar and set aside to pickle for between 30 minutes to 6 hours.
2. Heat 2 tsp oil, add the shallots, garlic, Cajun spice, paprika, and celery and fry for 2 minutes until vegetables are soft.
3. Mix the mince, parsley, and cooled onion mixture. Shape 4 burgers out of the mixture, put in the fridge for 15 minutes to rest.
4. Spray a non-stick pan with olive oil, then fry the burgers for 5 minutes a side, until golden brown and cooked through.
5. Stir together the mayonnaise and mustard.
6. Assemble the burgers by cutting the buns in half, spreading evenly with mustard mayo, place rocket and tomatoes on the bottom half. Place the burgers on top of the tomatoes and finish off with a small spoon of pickled onion and bun top. Serve hot.
7. Get the serviettes ready and enjoy.

Nutrition Info:
- Info420 calories,36g carbs,33g protein,698mg sodium,17g fat.

Ground Turkey Sloppy Joes

Servings:4
Cooking Time:x
Ingredients:

- 1 pound lean ground turkey
- 1 medium onion, peeled and diced
- 3 cloves garlic, peeled and minced
- 1 medium red bell pepper, seeded and diced
- 1 medium tomato, diced
- 1 can no-salt-added tomato sauce
- 1 can no-salt-added tomato paste
- ¼ cup apple cider vinegar
- 2 tablespoons light brown sugar
- 1 teaspoon dried oregano
- ½ teaspoon ground cumin
- ¼ teaspoon ground black pepper
- 4 Soft and Crusty No-Rise Rolls

Directions:
1. Place ground turkey, onion, and garlic in a large skillet over medium heat. Cook, stirring, for 5 minutes.
2. Add bell pepper, tomato, tomato sauce, tomato paste, vinegar, brown sugar, oregano, cumin, and black pepper and stir to combine. Reduce heat to medium-low and simmer for 20 minutes, stirring occasionally. Remove from heat.
3. Divide mixture evenly between rolls. Serve immediately.

Nutrition Info:
- InfoCalories 407,Fat 9g,Sodium 142mg,Carbohydrates 52g,Protein 30g

Crispy Turkey In Tomato Sauce

Servings: 4
Cooking Time: 20 Mins
Ingredients:

- 2 tbsp. olive oil
- ½ small onion, minced
- 2 tsp garlic, finely chopped
- 1 medium carrot, grated
- 1 large sweet red pepper, sliced
- 1 cup pink oyster mushrooms, sliced
- 1 tsp dried thyme
- 1 14.5-ounce low sodium can chopped tomatoes
- 17-ounces turkey breast - 4 breasts
- Sprig parsley to garnish

Directions:

1. First, make your tomato sauce by heating 1 tbsp. oil in a pan. Add in the onion, garlic, carrot, and pepper. Fry for about 1 minute. Then add in the dried thyme and oyster mushrooms. Lastly, add in the canned tomatoes, and simmer on low heat for about 7 minutes.
2. In a separate pan, fry off the turkey breasts in the remaining oil. Cook for about 3 minutes on each side until cooked through and a crisp brown outer layer is formed.
3. Add the turkey breasts and juices to the sauce and simmer for about 2 minutes to amalgamate the flavors.
4. Serve hot, garnished with a sprig of parsley.

Nutrition Info:

- Info225 calories,10g carbs,30g protein,67mg sodium,8g fat.

Turkey And Brown Rice–stuffed Peppers

Servings:4
Cooking Time:x
Ingredients:

- 4 large bell peppers
- 1 pound lean ground turkey
- 1 medium onion, peeled and diced
- 3 cloves garlic, peeled and minced
- 2 stalks celery, diced
- 2 cups cooked brown rice
- 1 can no-salt-added diced tomatoes
- 2 tablespoons no-salt-added tomato paste
- ¼ cup raisins
- 2 teaspoons ground cumin
- 1 teaspoon dried oregano
- ½ teaspoon ground cinnamon
- ½ teaspoon ground black pepper

Directions:

1. Preheat oven to 425°F. Lightly spray a 9" × 13" baking dish with nonstick cooking spray and set aside.
2. Trim about ½" off the top of each pepper and set tops aside. Carefully core and seed, leaving the peppers intact. Trim bottoms if necessary so that peppers sit flat. Set aside.
3. Heat a medium skillet over medium heat. Add ground turkey, onion, garlic, and celery and sauté for 5 minutes. Remove from heat. Stir in the remaining ingredients.
4. Fill each pepper with ¼ of the mixture, pressing firmly to pack. Stand peppers in the prepared baking dish, replace the pepper tops, and then cover dish tightly with foil. Place dish on middle rack in oven and bake until tender, 25–30 minutes.
5. Remove from oven and serve immediately.

Nutrition Info:

- InfoCalories 354,Fat 8g,Sodium 126mg,Carbohydrates 45g,Protein 27g

Cheesy Turkey Filled Pasta Shells

Servings: 2-3
Cooking Time: 50 Mins
Ingredients:

- 8 large individual pasta shells
- ½ tsp olive oil, plus extra in a spray bottle
- ¼ cup finely chopped red onion
- 1 tsp fresh garlic, minced
- 8-ounces turkey mince, lean
- 1 cup grated gouda cheese
- 1 ½ cups low fat cream cheese
- Black pepper to taste
- 2 tbsp. finely chopped parsley
- 8-ounces Swiss chard, de-stemmed and roughly chopped
- 1 ½ cups readymade Marinara sauce

Directions:

1. Bring a medium pot of water to a boil.
2. Preheat the oven to 375⁰F and spray a semi-deep casserole dish with olive oil.
3. Place the pasta shells in boiling water and cook for about 8 minutes. Drain and place on the greased casserole dish.
4. Heat the oil in a pan, and fry off the onion, with the garlic and black pepper to taste. Once the onions are soft, add in the turkey mince, and cook until it changes color completely, about 6 minutes. Add the Swiss chard in the last minutes and turn off the heat.
5. In a bowl, mix the cream cheese with all but 3 tbsp. Gouda. Add in the parsley and then the turkey mixture and mix well. Season with pepper to taste.
6. Place ½ cup of marinara sauce underneath the pasta shells in the casserole dish. Then fill them equally with the turkey mixture. Pour the rest of the marinara sauce over them and cover with grated cheese.
7. Bake covered for 25 minutes, uncover, and bake for another 5 minutes until the cheese browns nicely.
8. Serve hot and enjoy.

Nutrition Info:

- Info907 calories,73g carbs,70g protein,714mg sodium,39g fat.

Sloppy Toms

Servings:4
Cooking Time:x
Ingredients:

- 1 tablespoon canola oil
- 1 medium yellow onion, chopped
- 2 large celery ribs, cut into ½-inch dice
- 1 large green bell pepper, cored and cut into ½-inch dice
- 1¼ pounds ground turkey
- 1 can no-salt-added tomato sauce
- ½ cup no-salt-added tomato ketchup
- 1 tablespoon Worcestershire sauce
- 1 tablespoon balsamic vinegar
- 1 teaspoon kosher salt
- ½ teaspoon freshly ground black pepper
- 6 whole-wheat sandwich buns, toasted

Directions:

1. Heat the oil in a large nonstick skillet over medium heat. Add the onion, celery, and bell pepper and sauté, stirring occasionally, until softened, about 5 minutes. Move the vegetables to one side of the skillet. Add the ground turkey to the cleared side of the skillet and cook, stirring occasionally and breaking up the meat with the side of a wooden spoon, until the turkey loses its raw look, about 6 minutes. Mix the turkey and vegetables.
2. Stir in the tomato sauce, ketchup, Worcestershire sauce, vinegar, salt, and pepper and bring to a simmer. Reduce the heat to medium-low and simmer, stirring often, until slightly thickened, about 10 minutes.
3. For each serving, spoon ⅔cup of the turkey mixture onto half a bun on a plate, then cover with the top half of the bun. Serve hot.

Nutrition Info:

- Info222 calories,18 g protein,15 g carbohydrates,12 g fat,389 mg sodiu.

Classic Poached Chicken

Servings:2
Cooking Time:x
Ingredients:

- 2 chicken breast halves, with skin and bones
- 1 small onion, thinly sliced
- 2 sprigs of fresh parsley (optional)
- Pinch of dried thyme
- A few black peppercorns
- ½ bay leaf

Directions:

1. In a medium saucepan, place the chicken and onion and add enough water to cover by 1 inch. Bring to a simmer over high heat, skimming off any foam that rises to the surface.
2. Add the parsley (if using) and the thyme, peppercorns, and bay leaf. Reduce the heat to medium-low and simmer for 15 minutes. The chicken will not be completely cooked.
3. Remove from the heat and cover tightly. Let stand until the chicken is opaque when pierced in the thickest part with the tip of a knife, about 20 minutes. Transfer the chicken to a cutting board and let cool until easy to handle.
4. Pull off the skin and bones. Cover and refrigerate the meat for up to 2 days.

Nutrition Info:

- Info194 calories,33 g protein,4 g carbohydrates,4 g fat,183 mg sodiu.

Chicken, Black Bean, And Veggie Soft Tacos

Servings:6
Cooking Time:x
Ingredients:

- 1 package 5-inch corn tortillas
- 3 boneless, skinless chicken thighs
- 1⁄2 cup low-sodium chicken broth
- 1 medium carrot, diced
- 1 medium sweet potato, diced
- 1 medium onion, diced
- 1 medium bell pepper, diced
- 1 jalapeño pepper, minced
- 3 cloves garlic, minced
- 1 can no-salt-added black beans
- 1⁄2 cup corn kernels
- 2 tablespoons no-salt-added tomato paste
- 2 tablespoons Salt-Free Chili Seasoning
- 1⁄2 cup nonfat sour cream
- 1⁄4 cup chopped fresh cilantro

Directions:

1. Warm corn tortillas as desired; set aside.
2. Wash the chicken and cut into bite-sized pieces.
3. Heat a sauté pan over medium heat. Add the broth, carrot, and sweet potato, cover the pan, and cook for 5 minutes.
4. Add the chicken, onion, peppers, and garlic, cover, and cook for another 5 minutes, stirring once halfway through cooking time.
5. Add the beans with liquid, corn, tomato paste, and chili seasoning to the pan. Stir well and cook, stirring, for 5 minutes.
6. Remove from heat. Spoon filling into warm tortillas and garnish with sour cream and cilantro.
7. Serve immediately.

Nutrition Info:

- InfoCalories: 338,Fat: 3 g,Protein: 17 g,Sodium: 90 mg,Carbohydrates: 63 .

Fish And Seafood

Japanese Yellowfin Tuna

Servings: 2
Cooking Time: 2 Mins
Ingredients:

- 1 tsp olive oil
- ½ tsp minced fresh ginger
- Juice of 1 lime
- 2 tbsp. low sodium soy sauce
- 2 tbsp. wholegrain mustard
- 10-ounces yellowfin tuna, A-grade
- 4 spring onions, finely sliced

Directions:
1. Make the marinade first by combining the ginger, lime juice, 1 tbsp. soy sauce and mustard in a bowl. Dunk the steaks into this marinade, coating both sides well.
2. Heat a large non-stick pan and add the olive oil. Sear the tuna in the pan for 1 minute per side. The fish should still be rare on the inside.
3. Serve hot, sliced into ¼-inch slices, and garnished with spring onions and remaining soy sauce on the side.

Nutrition Info:

- Info126 calories,3g carbs,18g protein,313mg sodium,5g fat.

Salmon Cakes

Servings:6
Cooking Time:x
Ingredients:

- 1 can no-salt-added boneless salmon, drained
- 4 tablespoons Salt-Free Mayonnaise
- ½ cup salt-free bread crumbs
- 1 small onion, peeled and minced
- 1 small bell pepper, seeded and minced
- 1 large egg white
- 1 teaspoon dried herbes de Provence
- ½ teaspoon ground paprika
- ¼ teaspoon ground mustard
- ⅛ teaspoon celery seed
- ¼ teaspoon ground black pepper

Directions:
1. Preheat oven to 400°F. Spray a baking sheet lightly with nonstick cooking spray and set aside.
2. Place all ingredients in a large bowl. Mix using a spoon or your hands. Divide mixture into 6 equal portions and shape into patties.
3. Place patties on the prepared baking sheet. Place baking sheet on middle rack in oven and bake for 10 minutes. Remove from oven, gently flip, and return to oven to bake 5 minutes more.
4. Remove from oven and serve immediately.

Nutrition Info:

- InfoCalories 202,Fat 11g,Sodium 68mg,Carbohydrates 8g,Protein 16g

Cod With Grapefruit, Avocado, And Fennel Salad

Servings:4
Cooking Time:x
Ingredients:

- Grapefruit, Avocado, and Fennel Salad
- 1 small fennel bulb
- 2 tablespoons fresh lemon juice
- 1 tablespoon extra-virgin olive oil
- ¼ teaspoon kosher salt
- ¼ teaspoon freshly ground black pepper
- 1 ripe avocado, pitted, peeled, and cut into ½-inch dice
- 1 pink or red grapefruit, peel removed, cut between the membranes into segments
- Cod
- 2 teaspoons olive oil
- 4 cod fillets

Directions:

1. To make the salad: Cut the fennel in half lengthwise. If the fronds are attached, cut them off and reserve. Cut out and discard the triangular core at the base of the bulb. Cut one fennel half crosswise into thin half-moons. Reserve the remaining fennel half and stalks for another use.
2. In a medium bowl, whisk together the lemon juice and oil, and season with salt and pepper. Add the fennel, avocado, and grapefruit and mix gently. Set aside while preparing the cod.
3. To prepare the cod: Heat the oil in a large nonstick skillet over medium heat. Add the cod and cover. Cook until the undersides are golden, about 3 minutes. Turn and cook, uncovered, adjusting the heat as needed, until the other side of each fillet is golden brown and the cod looks barely opaque when flaked in the center with the tip of a knife, about 3 minutes more.
4. Divide the fennel salad among four dinner plates. Top each with a cod fillet and serve immediately.

Nutrition Info:

- Info270 calories,27 g protein,14 g carbohydrates,12 g fat,232 mg sodium,1 fat.

Roasted Salmon Fillets With Basil Drizzle

Servings:4
Cooking Time:x
Ingredients:

- Salmon
- Olive oil in a pump sprayer
- 4 skinless salmon fillets
- ¼ teaspoon kosher salt
- ¼ teaspoon freshly ground black pepper
- Basil Drizzle
- 1 clove garlic, peeled
- ½ cup packed fresh basil leaves
- 3 tablespoons coarsely chopped fresh parsley leaves
- 2 tablespoons water
- 1 tablespoon balsamic vinegar
- Pinch of kosher salt
- Pinch of freshly ground black pepper
- ¼ cup extra-virgin olive oil

Directions:

1. To prepare the salmon: Preheat the oven to 400°F. Spray a 9 × 13-inch baking dish with oil.
2. Place the salmon fillets in the baking dish, spray with oil, and season with the salt and pepper. Roast until the salmon looks barely opaque when prodded in the thickest part with the tip of a knife, about 10 minutes.
3. Meanwhile, make the basil drizzle: With a food processor running, drop the garlic clove through the feed tube to mince the garlic. (Or drop the garlic through the hole in the lid of a blender.) Stop the food processor or blender, add the basil, parsley, water, vinegar, salt, and pepper, and pulse a few times to chop the herbs. With the motor running, gradually add the oil. Pour the drizzle mixture into a small bowl.
4. Using a metal spatula, transfer the fillets to dinner plates and drizzle with equal amounts of the basil mixture. Serve hot.

Nutrition Info:

- Info370 calories,34 g protein,1 g carbohydrates,24 g fat,250 mg sodiu.

Tuna With Fennel And Potatoes

Servings:4
Cooking Time:x
Ingredients:

- Vegetables
- 1 tablespoon olive oil, plus more in a pump sprayer
- 1 head fennel
- 3 medium potatoes, scrubbed but unpeeled, cut in halves and then crosswise into ¼-inch-thick slices
- 1 large red bell pepper, cored and cut into ¼-inch-wide strips
- 4 cloves garlic, chopped
- Freshly grated zest of 1 lemon
- 1 teaspoon kosher salt
- ½ teaspoon crushed hot red pepper
- 2 tablespoons freshly grated Parmesan cheese
- Tuna
- Olive oil in a pump sprayer
- 4 tuna steaks, about 1 inch thick
- ½ teaspoon freshly ground black pepper
- Lemon wedges, for serving

Directions:
1. Preheat the oven to 400°F.
2. To prepare the vegetables: Spray a 9 × 13-inch baking dish with oil. Cut the fronds (leaves) off the fennel. Chop 2 tablespoons of fennel fronds and reserve. Cut the fennel head in half lengthwise, and cut out the thick triangular core at the bottom of the head. Cut the head and stalks crosswise into ¼- to ½-inch-wide strips.
3. Heat the 1 tablespoon oil in a large nonstick skillet over medium-high heat. Add the potatoes and cook, stirring occasionally, until they begin to soften around the edges, about 5 minutes. Stir in the fennel, bell pepper, garlic, lemon zest, salt, and hot pepper. Spread in the baking dish. Bake, stirring occasionally, until the potatoes are tender, about 30 minutes. During the last 5 minutes, sprinkle with the Parmesan. Remove from the oven and let stand while preparing the tuna.
4. To prepare the tuna: Wipe the skillet clean with paper towels. Spray the skillet with oil and heat over medium-high heat. Season the tuna with the pepper. Place the tuna steaks in the skillet and cook until the undersides are seared, about 2 minutes. Flip the tuna and cook until the other sides are seared, about 2 minutes more for rare tuna.
5. Divide the vegetables equally among four dinner plates, and top each with a tuna steak. Sprinkle with the reserved chopped fronds. Serve hot, with the lemon wedges.

Nutrition Info:
- Info335 calories,40 g protein,29 g carbohydrates,5 g fat,372 mg sodiu.

Sea Scallops And Vegetables With Ginger Sauce

Servings:4
Cooking Time:x
Ingredients:

- 1 pound sea scallops, each cut in half horizontally
- ¾ cup low-sodium chicken broth
- 1 tablespoon reduced-sodium soy sauce
- 1 tablespoon rice vinegar
- ¼ teaspoon crushed hot red pepper
- 2 teaspoons cornstarch
- 1 tablespoon canola or vegetable oil
- 8 ounces sugar snap peas, trimmed
- 1 large red bell pepper, cored and cut into 2 × ¼-inch strips
- 2 scallions, white and green parts, 1 minced and 1 finely chopped
- 1½ tablespoons peeled and minced fresh ginger
- 2 cloves garlic, minced

Directions:
1. Bring a medium saucepan of water to a boil over high heat. Add the scallops and cook just until they turn opaque around the edges, about 30 seconds. Drain.
2. In a glass measuring cup, combine the broth, soy sauce, vinegar, and hot pepper. Sprinkle in the cornstarch and stir with a fork until dissolved. Set aside.
3. Heat a large wok or skillet over high heat. Drizzle in the oil, tilting the wok to coat the entire surface. Add the sugar snap peas and bell pepper and stir-fry until beginning to soften, about 1 minute. Stir in the minced scallion, ginger, and garlic and stir-fry until fragrant, about 30 seconds. Add the scallops and broth mixture and bring to a boil, stirring often. Cook until the scallops are opaque throughout and the sauce is thickened, about 1 minute.
4. Divide the scallop mixture evenly among four bowls, sprinkle with the chopped scallion, and serve hot.

Nutrition Info:
- Info169 calories,17 g protein,14 g carbohydrates,4 g fat,763 mg sodiu.

Halibut With Spring Vegetables

Servings:4
Cooking Time:x
Ingredients:

- 8 baby red-skinned potatoes, scrubbed but unpeeled, cut in halves
- 32 baby carrots, preferably not baby-cut carrots, trimmed
- 1 tablespoon unsalted butter
- 1 cup chopped leeks, white and pale green parts only
- 1 cup Homemade Chicken Broth (here) or canned low-sodium chicken broth
- ½ cup water
- ¼ cup dry vermouth or white wine
- 4 skinless halibut fillets
- ¼ teaspoon kosher salt
- ¼ teaspoon freshly ground black pepper
- Finely chopped fresh chives, parsley, or a combination, for serving
- Lemon wedges, for serving

Directions:

1. Bring a medium saucepan of water to a boil over high heat. Add the potatoes, reduce heat to medium, and cook at a steady simmer for 5 minutes. Add the carrots and cook until the vegetables are almost, but not quite, tender when pierced with the tip of a small, sharp knife, about 3 minutes more. Drain and rinse under cold running water.
2. Melt the butter in a large skillet over medium heat. Add the leeks and cover. Cook, stirring occasionally, until tender, about 5 minutes. Add the broth, water, and vermouth and bring to a simmer. Reduce the heat to medium-low, cover partially with the lid, and simmer for 5 minutes to blend the flavors.
3. Spread the potatoes and carrots in the skillet in a single layer. Arrange the halibut fillets on the vegetables and season with the salt and pepper. Cover tightly and simmer until the vegetables are tender and the halibut is opaque in the center when pierced with the tip of a small, sharp knife, 10 to 12 minutes.
4. Divide the vegetables and broth evenly among four deep soup bowls. Top each with a halibut fillet and sprinkle with the herbs. Add the lemon wedges and serve hot.

Nutrition Info:

- Info256 calories,29 g protein,19 g carbohydrates,5 g fat,270 mg sodiu.

Haddock Tacos With Mexican Slaw

Servings: 6
Cooking Time: 8 Mins
Ingredients:

- Olive oil in a spray bottle
- 12-ounces cabbage cut chiffonade style
- 2 tbsp. low fat sour cream
- 2 tbsp. fresh lime juice
- Zest of 1 lime
- 1 small red pepper, sliced
- 2 spring onions finely sliced
- 2 tbsp. chopped fresh coriander, plus extra to garnish
- 2 tbsp. minced fresh mint
- 24-ounces haddock fillets
- 2 tsp cayenne pepper
- 2 tbsp. fresh lime juice
- 12 6-inch hard shell corn tacos
- 2 limes cut into quarters to serve

Directions:

1. Mix the sour cream, lime juice and zest in a large bowl. Add the cabbage, red pepper, onions, mint, and coriander and combine.
2. In a separate bowl, combine the other 2 tbsp. lime juice and cayenne pepper. Pour this mixture over the fish fillets and let stand in the fridge for 2 minutes.
3. Oil a non-stick pan and fry the haddock until flaky and cooked through. About 9 minutes a side.
4. Place in a bowl and pull apart into pieces. Mix in the cabbage mixture.
5. Warm the tacos in oven for about 2 minutes, then spoon the fish mixture into them and serve with a wedge of lime and fresh coriander to garnish.

Nutrition Info:

- Info247 calories,29g carbs,24g protein,308mg sodium,4g fat.

Brown Rice Paella With Cod, Shrimp, And Asparagus

Servings:6
Cooking Time:x
Ingredients:

- 8 ounces asparagus, woody stems discarded, cut into 1-inch lengths
- 1 tablespoon olive oil
- 1 medium yellow onion, chopped
- 1 medium red bell pepper, cored and cut into ½-inch dice
- 2 cloves garlic, minced
- 1 cup brown rice
- 2 cups Homemade Chicken Broth (here) or canned low-sodium chicken broth
- 1 can no-salt-added diced tomatoes, drained
- ½ cup water
- 1 teaspoon dried oregano
- ½ teaspoon crushed hot red pepper
- ¼ teaspoon crushed saffron threads
- 12 ounces cod fillets, cut into 1-inch pieces
- 8 ounces large shrimp, peeled and deveined
- Lemon wedges, for serving

Directions:

1. Bring a small saucepan of water to a boil over high heat. Add the asparagus and cook until crisp and bright green, about 2 minutes. (It will finish cooking later.) Drain, rinse under cold running water, and drain again. Set aside.
2. Heat the oil in a medium Dutch oven or flameproof casserole over medium heat. Add the onion, bell pepper, and garlic and cook, stirring occasionally, until softened, about 3 minutes. Stir in the brown rice. Add the broth, tomatoes, water, oregano, hot pepper, and saffron and bring to a boil. Reduce the heat to medium-low and simmer, covered, until the rice has almost completely absorbed the liquid, about 40 minutes.
3. Add the cod, shrimp, and asparagus to the Dutch oven. Cover and cook until the cod is opaque throughout, about 5 minutes. Remove from the heat and uncover. Let stand for 3 minutes. Serve hot, with the lemon wedges.

Nutrition Info:

- Info266 calories,21 g protein,35 g carbohydrates,5 g fat,302 mg sodiu.

Shrimp With Corn Hash

Servings:4
Cooking Time:x
Ingredients:

- 4 teaspoons olive oil
- 1 pound large shrimp, peeled and deveined
- ½ cup chopped red onion
- ½ medium red bell pepper, seeded and cut into ½-inch dice
- 1½ cups fresh corn kernels, cut from 2 large ears of corn
- 1 cup halved cherry or grape tomatoes
- ¼ teaspoon crushed hot red pepper
- ¼ cup water
- 1 tablespoon fresh lemon juice
- 2 tablespoons coarsely chopped fresh basil

Directions:

1. Heat 2 teaspoons of the oil in a large nonstick skillet over medium-high heat. Add the shrimp and cook, stirring occasionally, until it is opaque throughout, 3 to 5 minutes. Transfer to a plate.
2. Heat the remaining 2 teaspoons oil in the skillet over medium-high heat. Add the onion and bell pepper and cook, stirring often, until softened, about 1 minute. Add the corn, tomatoes, and hot pepper and cover. Cook, stirring occasionally, until these vegetables are heated through, about 3 minutes.
3. Add the shrimp and reheat, stirring often, about 1 minute. Stir in the water and lemon juice and cook, scraping up any browned bits in the pan with a wooden spoon. Transfer to a serving bowl and sprinkle with the basil. Serve hot.

Nutrition Info:

- Info195 calories,18 g protein,18 g carbohydrates,6 g fat,647 mg sodiu.

Fish Tacos With Lime-cilantro Slaw

Servings:6
Cooking Time:x
Ingredients:
- Fish
- 2 tablespoons fresh lime juice
- 2 teaspoons chili powder
- 1½ pounds cod fillets
- Slaw
- Freshly grated zest of 1 lime
- 2 tablespoons fresh lime juice
- 2 tablespoons light mayonnaise
- 1 bag coleslaw mix
- 2 plum (Roma) tomatoes, seeded and cut into ½-inch dice
- 2 scallions, white and green parts, finely chopped
- 2 tablespoons finely chopped fresh cilantro
- ½ teaspoon kosher salt
- Olive oil in a pump sprayer
- 12 corn tortillas, warmed
- Lime wedges, for serving

Directions:
1. To prepare the fish: Whisk together the lime juice and chili powder in a shallow glass or ceramic baking dish. Add the cod and turn to coat. Cover and refrigerate while making the slaw.
2. To make the slaw: In a large bowl, whisk together the lime zest and juice and mayonnaise. Add the coleslaw mix, tomatoes, scallions, cilantro, and salt and mix well. Set aside.
3. Spray a large nonstick skillet with oil and heat over medium-high heat. Remove the fish from the baking dish, letting the excess juice drip back into the dish. Place in the skillet and cook, turning occasionally, until opaque when flaked in the thickest part with the tip of a knife, about 8 minutes. Transfer to a serving bowl and flake into large chunks with a fork.
4. For each serving, spoon some fish and slaw on a tortilla, then fold and eat, with a squeeze of lime juice, if you wish.

Nutrition Info:
- Info247 calories,24 g protein,29 g carbohydrates,4 g fat,308 mg sodiu.

Roasted Steelhead Trout With Grapefruit Sauce

Servings:4
Cooking Time:x
Ingredients:
- 1 pound steelhead trout
- 3 teaspoons olive oil, divided
- Freshly ground black pepper, to taste
- 2 medium ruby red grapefruits
- 1 shallot, minced
- 1 clove garlic, minced
- 1 teaspoon minced fresh ginger
- 2 teaspoons agave nectar
- 1⁄8 teaspoon ground cayenne pepper
- 2 tablespoons thinly sliced fresh basil

Directions:
1. Preheat the oven to 350°F. Place the steelhead trout in a baking dish, brush with 2 teaspoons olive oil, and season with freshly ground black pepper to taste. Place the pan on the middle rack in the oven and roast for 15 minutes.
2. To prepare the sauce, cut the top and bottom off one of the grapefruits. Stand on one end and cut down to remove the white pith and peel. Use a sharp knife to remove each grapefruit segment from its membrane. Cut the segments in half and set aside. Juice the other grapefruit and set aside.
3. Heat the remaining teaspoon of olive oil in a saucepan over medium heat. Add the shallot and garlic and sauté for 2 minutes.
4. Add the ginger, grapefruit juice, agave nectar, and cayenne and stir to combine. Bring to a simmer, then cook until reduced by half, about 10 minutes.
5. Remove saucepan from heat. Stir in the grapefruit and basil.
6. Remove trout from oven. Slice into 4 portions, garnish with sauce, and serve immediately.

Nutrition Info:
- InfoCalories: 250,Fat: 7 g,Protein: 24 g,Sodium: 36 mg,Carbohydrates: 22 .

Summer Salmon Parcels

Servings: 4
Cooking Time: 20 Mins
Ingredients:

- 4 6-ounce salmon fillets, without skin
- 2 Cara-Cara oranges, peeled and cut into thin discs
- 2 cups julienne baby marrows
- 1 small onion, sliced
- 2 cups sliced acorn squash,
- Black pepper to taste
- Juice of 1 lemon plus extra to taste
- 1 tbsp. olive oil
- 2 tsp dried thyme
- 4 sprigs fresh thyme
- Tinfoil

Directions:

1. Cut out tinfoil parcels about 2 inches longer than the salmon fillets.
2. Preheat the oven to 400ºF.
3. Layer the vegetables on the left side of each tinfoil parcel, dividing them equally. Layer them in the following order: acorn squash, baby marrow, onion, orange. Lastly, place the fish fillets on top.
4. Whisk the lemon juice, olive oil and dried thyme together. Pour this equally over each fish fillet, and then top the fillets with a thyme sprig.
5. Close over the parcels, pulling the foil over from the right and sealing the edges well so that the juices can't escape.
6. Place parcels on a baking tray and cook for about 20 minutes until the fish is done.
7. To serve, carefully place the vegetables and fish on a plate attractively and spoon the remaining juices over the top.
8. Enjoy hot.

Nutrition Info:

- Info309 calories,18g carbs,37g protein,279mg sodium,11g fat.

Cajun Crusted Trout

Servings: 4
Cooking Time: 15 Mins
Ingredients:

- ¼ tsp chili powder
- 1 tsp treacle sugar
- 1 tsp brown onion powder
- 1 tsp paprika powder
- 2 tsp dried parsley
- 1 tsp dried oregano
- 1 tsp garlic powder
- 1 tsp ground cumin
- Black pepper to taste
- 17 ounces broccoli florets
- 4 6-ounce rainbow trout fillets
- 1 tsp olive oil
- 1 lemon, cut into 4 pieces

Directions:

1. Make the crust for the fish by mixing all the dried spices and herbs in a bowl.
2. Lightly oil the fish fillets and then pat the spice crust onto them evenly. Place them on a well-oiled baking tray.
3. Preheat the oven to 425ºF and lightly oil a baking tray.
4. Dress the broccoli with a little olive oil and pepper and place on the second oiled baking tray.
5. Bake both trays in the oven at the same time, for about 12-15 minutes, or until the fish and broccoli are superbly cooked. The trout should pull apart effortlessly and have a crisp, dark crust.
6. Serve with lemon quarters for squeezing.

Nutrition Info:

- Info280 calories,10g carbs,38g protein,227mg sodium,11g fat.

Spicy Tilapia With Pineapple Relish

Servings:4
Cooking Time:x
Ingredients:

- 1/2 medium pineapple, diced
- 1 small red onion, diced
- 1 small tomato, diced
- 1 jalapeño pepper, minced
- 2 cloves garlic, minced
- 2 tablespoons plain unflavored rice vinegar
- 2 tablespoons chopped fresh cilantro
- 2 teaspoons canola oil
- 1 teaspoon salt-free Cajun seasoning
- 1/4 teaspoon dried red pepper flakes
- 1 pound boneless tilapia fillet

Directions:

1. Combine pineapple, onion, tomato, jalapeño, and garlic in a mixing bowl. Add the vinegar and cilantro and stir to combine.
2. Heat oil in a large sauté pan over medium-high heat.
3. Combine Cajun seasoning and red pepper flakes in a small bowl and sprinkle evenly over the fish. Place fish in pan and cook for 2 minutes per side, or until fish flakes easily when tested with a fork.
4. Remove from heat and serve immediately, dividing the fish into 4 portions and plating each with a quarter of the pineapple relish.

Nutrition Info:

- InfoCalories: 220,Fat: 4 g,Protein: 24 g,Sodium: 68 mg,Carbohydrates: 22 .

Freshwater Fish Casserole

Servings: 2
Cooking Time: 15 Min
Ingredients:

- 2 tbsp. fresh lemon juice
- 4 tbsp. olive oil
- Black pepper to taste
- 1 tbsp. finely chopped fresh garlic
- 2 tbsp. chopped flat-leaf parsley
- 1 tbsp. finely chopped thyme
- 2 tbsp. finely chopped white onion
- 1 cup Butternut squash, peeled and largely diced
- 2 cups broccoli florets
- 1 cup zucchini, quartered
- 4 4-ounce tilapia fillets
- 2 tbsp. finely grated pecorino cheese
- 5-ounces fresh rocket
- 2 sprigs parsley to serve

Directions:

1. First, make your dressing for the fish by combining 2 tbsp. olive oil with the lemon juice, black pepper, herbs, garlic, and white onion. Set aside.
2. Preheat the oven to 400ºF.
3. Next, oil a large casserole dish with olive oil and place the remaining cut veg in it. Drizzle 1 tbsp. oil over them and toss to coat them evenly.
4. Make space for the four fish fillets and pour a small amount of the fish dressing into these spaces. Then place the fillets on top of the dressing and drizzle the remaining dressing over the fish.
5. Bake the casserole in the oven for about 15 minutes until the fish is cooked perfectly and flakes well.
6. To serve, dress the rocket with 2 tsp olive oil, black pepper, and the pecorino cheese.
7. Place the rocket mixture onto plates, with the fish fillets next to it. Spoon the roast veg over the rocket and serve immediately garnished with a sprig of parsley.

Nutrition Info:

- Info244 calories,9g carbs,29g protein,208mg sodium,13g fat.

Cheesy Shrimp Pasta

Servings: 2
Cooking Time: 20 Mins
Ingredients:

- 4 ounces penne pasta
- 2 tsp unsalted butter
- 1 tbsp. corn flour
- 2 tbsp. grated mature cheddar
- 1 cup low fat milk
- ¼ cup grated pecorino cheese
- Black pepper to taste
- 1 tbsp. olive oil
- 12 large, pre-cooked frozen shrimp, peeled and deveined
- 1 cup frozen edamame beans
- ½ cup chopped pecans
- ½ tsp mixed Italian herbs

Directions:
1. Bring a medium pot of water to a boil, then add the penne and cook at a fast boil for about 8 minutes.
2. Next, make your sauce. Melt the butter in a small pot. Once melted, whisk in the corn flour, making sure there are no lumps. Gradually add the milk, whisking all the time. Bring to a boil and stir until the sauce thickens. Then add black pepper to taste and add the grated cheddar cheese. Add 3 tbsp. parmesan and stir until the cheese melts. Cover to keep warm.
3. At this point, fry up your other ingredients by heating the olive oil in a pan, add the shrimp, edamame beans and pecans and fry for 1 minute. Add the Italian herbs and fry for a further 3 minutes until all the ingredients are hot all the way through.
4. Drain and rinse the pasta in hot water, then throw it into the cheesy sauce. Stir well.
5. Spoon the pasta into the serving bowls and cascade the shrimp mixture over the top to serve.
6. Enjoy hot.

Nutrition Info:
- Info673 calories,64g carbs,31g protein,653mg sodium,34g fat.

Healthy Fish And Chips

Servings:4
Cooking Time:x
Ingredients:

- 2 tablespoons unbleached all-purpose flour
- 2 tablespoons white whole-wheat flour
- Freshly ground black pepper, to taste
- 2 egg whites
- 2 cups salt-free bread crumbs or panko
- 1 tablespoon dried herbs (a single herb or mix of favorites, such as parsley, dill, thyme, etc.)
- 1 pound white-fleshed fish cut into 4 fillets
- 4 large potatoes, scrubbed
- 3 tablespoons olive oil
- Freshly ground black pepper, to taste

Directions:
1. Preheat oven to 425°F. Cover a large baking sheet with foil and set aside.
2. Measure the flours into a wide shallow bowl, add black pepper, and whisk to combine.
3. Place the egg whites into a second shallow bowl.
4. Place bread crumbs in a large plastic bag. Add herbs, seal bag, and shake well.
5. Cut the fish fillets in half, yielding 8 pieces total. Dredge each fillet completely in the seasoned flour, then dip in egg, coating completely.
6. Place the moistened fillet into the plastic bag, seal, and shake gently to coat. Once the fillet is totally coated, carefully remove from bag and place on the baking sheet. Repeat process until all pieces are battered. Place the tray of fish in the refrigerator.
7. Place a piece of parchment on a baking sheet. Cut each potato into 8 equal wedges. Arrange the wedges on the baking sheet and brush both sides lightly with oil. Season, to taste, with freshly ground black pepper.
8. Place baking sheet on the middle rack in the oven and bake for 15 minutes. Remove from oven and flip potatoes over. Return to middle rack in oven.
9. Remove the fish from the fridge and place on the top rack in the oven. Bake potatoes and fish for 15 minutes, until both are crispy and brown. Remove from oven and serve immediately.

Nutrition Info:
- InfoCalories: 534,Fat: 13 g,Protein: 38 g,Sodium: 142 mg,Carbohydrates: 65 .

Seafood Paella With Green Veg

Servings:6
Cooking Time: 50 Mins
Ingredients:

- 2 small fresh paprika peppers, diced
- 1 white onion, finely chopped
- 2 tsp minced fresh garlic
- 3 tbsp. chorizo sausage, finely chopped
- 1 tsp dried smoked paprika
- 1 tsp finely chopped fresh rosemary
- 1 tbsp. olive oil
- 1 cup brown rice
- 1 14.5-ounce can chopped tomatoes, low sodium
- 2 cups low sodium chicken stock
- ½ cup water
- 1 tsp dried mixed Italian herbs
- ½ tsp dried chili powder
- ¼ tsp crushed dried saffron
- 12 ounces haddock fillets, cut into cubes
- 8 ounces shrimp, peeled and deveined
- 8 ounces green beans, topped and tailed and cut in half
- 2 lemons, cut into wedges for serving

Directions:

1. Heat the olive oil in a deep bottomed paella pan, then add the onions, fresh paprika, and garlic. Fry for 1 minute, then add the chorizo, smoked paprika and rosemary and fry for a further minute.
2. Add the brown rice and stir, then add the tomatoes, stock, herbs and spices, and water. Cover the pan with a lid and simmer on a low heat for about 40 minutes, or until the rice is al dente.
3. Add in the fish, shrimps and cut green beans and cook for a further 5 minutes, until the fish is cooked through and the flavors have mixed in well.
4. Let the mixture rest for 3 minutes to settle the ingredients, then serve hot with lemon quarters.

Nutrition Info:

- Info266 calories,35g carbs,21g protein,301mg sodium,5g fat.

Ahi Tuna With Grape Tomato Salsa

Servings:4
Cooking Time:x
Ingredients:

- 2 cups grape tomatoes, halved
- 1/4 cup finely diced onion
- 1/4 cup finely diced green bell pepper
- 1 clove garlic, minced
- 1 tablespoon apple cider vinegar
- 1 tablespoon chopped fresh cilantro
- 1/2 teaspoon ground cumin
- 1/4 teaspoon ground coriander
- 1/4 teaspoon freshly ground black pepper
- 1/8 teaspoon dried red pepper flakes
- 1 pound ahi (yellowfin) tuna, cut into 4 steaks
- 1 tablespoon olive oil
- Freshly ground black pepper, to taste

Directions:

1. To make the salsa, add the tomatoes, onion, bell pepper, garlic, vinegar, cilantro, cumin, coriander, black pepper, and pepper flakes into a mixing bowl and stir well to combine. Set aside. Salsa can be made ahead and refrigerated until time to cook.
2. To cook the tuna, preheat broiler. Place the tuna steaks on a broiler pan or in a shallow baking dish, brush lightly with olive oil, and sprinkle with freshly ground black pepper, to taste. Place on top rack in oven and broil for 4 minutes.
3. Remove pan from oven, carefully flip steaks, brush with remaining oil, sprinkle additional pepper, to taste, and return to oven. Broil for another 4 minutes.
4. Remove from oven. Plate each steak with 1/4 of the tomato salsa. Serve immediately.

Nutrition Info:

- InfoCalories: 174,Fat: 4 g,Protein: 27 g,Sodium: 48 mg,Carbohydrates: 4 .

Vegan And Vegetarian

Coconut Cauliflower Curry

Servings:6
Cooking Time:x
Ingredients:

- 1 tablespoon canola oil
- 1 medium onion, diced
- 6 cloves garlic, minced
- 1 tablespoon minced fresh ginger
- 1 tablespoon salt-free garam masala
- 1 teaspoon ground turmeric
- 2 tablespoons salt-free tomato paste
- 2 cups low-sodium vegetable broth
- 1 cup light coconut milk
- 1 head cauliflower, cut into florets
- 3 medium potatoes or sweet potatoes, diced
- 2 medium carrots, sliced
- 1 can no-salt-added diced tomatoes
- 1 1/2 cups fresh or frozen peas
- 1/2 teaspoon freshly ground black pepper
- 1/4 cup chopped fresh cilantro

Directions:

1. Heat oil in a stockpot over medium heat. Add onion, garlic, and ginger and cook, stirring, for 5 minutes.
2. Add the garam masala and turmeric and sauté until fragrant, roughly 30 seconds to 1 minute.
3. Stir in the tomato paste, broth, coconut milk, cauliflower, potatoes, carrots, and tomatoes with juice and stir well to combine. Raise heat slightly and bring to a boil. Once boiling, lower heat to medium-low, cover, and simmer for 20 minutes.
4. Stir in the peas and black pepper and cook 2–3 minutes more.
5. Remove from heat and stir in the cilantro. Serve immediately.

Nutrition Info:

- InfoCalories: 178,Fat: 6 g,Protein: 5 g,Sodium: 117 mg,Carbohydrates: 27 .

30-minute Vegetarian Pizza

Servings:4
Cooking Time:x
Ingredients:

- 1 cup white whole-wheat flour
- 1 teaspoon all-purpose salt-free seasoning
- 1 teaspoon salt-free Italian seasoning
- 1/2 teaspoon garlic powder
- 2 egg whites
- 2/3 cup low-fat milk
- 2 teaspoons olive oil
- 1 small eggplant, peeled and diced
- 1 medium onion, diced
- 1/2 cup no-salt-added pasta sauce
- 1 small bell pepper, diced
- 1 small tomato, diced
- 1 cup sliced mushrooms
- 1/2 cup chopped fresh broccoli
- 2 cloves garlic, minced
- 2 tablespoons chopped fresh basil
- 1/2 cup shredded Swiss cheese

Directions:

1. Preheat oven to 425°F. Grease and flour a 12-inch nonstick pizza pan and set aside.
2. Place the flour and seasonings into a mixing bowl and whisk well to combine. Add the egg whites and milk and stir well. Pour batter into the prepared pizza pan and set aside.
3. Place a large skillet over medium heat. Add the diced eggplant and onion and cook, stirring, for 5 minutes.
4. Remove from heat and spoon mixture evenly over the batter in the pan. Place pan on middle rack in oven and bake for 20 minutes.
5. Once crust is baked spread pasta sauce evenly over crust. Top pizza with bell pepper, tomato, mushrooms, broccoli, garlic, and basil. Sprinkle the Swiss cheese evenly over top.
6. Return pan to oven and bake 3–5 minutes, until cheese has melted.
7. Remove pizza from oven. Gently remove from pan and cut into 8 slices. Serve immediately.

Nutrition Info:

- InfoCalories: 242,Fat: 7 g,Protein: 13 g,Sodium: 82 mg,Carbohydrates: 34 .

Coconut Collards With Sweet Potatoes And Black Beans

Servings:8
Cooking Time: 23 Minutes
Ingredients:

- 1 tablespoon olive oil (optional, see note in steps)
- 1 medium onion, chopped
- 4 cloves garlic, minced
- 2 medium carrots, sliced
- 2 medium stalks celery, sliced
- 1 medium red bell pepper, diced
- 2 medium sweet potatoes, peeled and cubed
- 1 pound collard greens, chopped
- 1 can no-salt-added diced tomatoes, with juice
- 1 can light coconut milk, shaken well
- 1 can no-salt-added black beans, drained and rinsed
- 4 tablespoons no-salt-added tomato paste
- 1 tablespoon Thai Red Curry Paste
- Juice of 2 fresh limes
- 1 1/2 teaspoons ground cumin
- 1 1/2 teaspoons ground sweet paprika
- 1/4 teaspoon ground allspice
- Freshly ground black pepper, to taste

Directions:

1. Measure the olive oil into a stockpot, or if you prefer, coat bottom of pan with a thin layer of water. Place pot over medium heat. Add the onion, garlic, carrots, celery, bell pepper, and sweet potatoes and cook, stirring, 3 minutes.
2. Add the remaining ingredients and stir well to combine. Cover and simmer over medium heat, stirring frequently, 10 minutes.
3. Reduce heat to medium-low to low, and continue to simmer, stirring frequently, 5–10 minutes more. Keep checking to make sure the mixture isn't cooking too fast or beginning to stick and burn. Dish is ready when the sweet potatoes are fork tender.
4. Remove from heat and serve immediately over cooked rice, quinoa, or your favorite whole grain.

Nutrition Info:

- InfoCalories: 208,Fat: 6 g,Protein: 8 g,Sodium: 102 ml,Carbohydrates: 30 .

Marinara Sauce

Servings:1
Cooking Time:x
Ingredients:

- 1 tablespoon olive oil
- 1 medium onion, finely chopped
- 2 medium carrots, finely chopped
- 2 medium celery ribs, finely chopped
- 1 clove garlic, minced
- 1 can no-salt-added crushed tomatoes
- ¾ cup water
- 2 tablespoons balsamic vinegar
- 2 teaspoons Italian Seasoning (here)
- 1 bay leaf

Directions:

1. Heat the oil in a medium saucepan over medium heat. Add the onion, carrots, celery, and garlic and cover. Cook, stirring occasionally, until tender, about 6 minutes. Stir in the tomatoes, water, vinegar, Italian Seasoning, and bay leaf and bring to a simmer. Reduce the heat to medium-low, uncover, and simmer, stirring occasionally, until lightly thickened, about 1 hour. Remove the bay leaf.

Nutrition Info:

- Info59 calories,1 g protein,10 g carbohydrates,2 g fat,61 mg sodiu.

Summer Vegetable Risotto

Servings:4
Cooking Time:x
Ingredients:

- 4 teaspoons olive oil
- 2 medium zucchini, cut into ½-inch dice
- 1 medium yellow onion, chopped
- 1 clove garlic, minced
- 1 cup halved cherry or grape tomatoes
- ½ teaspoon kosher salt
- ¼ teaspoon freshly ground black pepper
- 2½ cups Homemade Chicken Broth (here) or canned low-sodium chicken broth
- 2½ cups water
- 1 cup Italian rice for risotto, such as arborio
- 2 tablespoons finely chopped fresh oregano
- Freshly grated zest of 1 lemon
- 4 tablespoons freshly grated Parmesan cheese, for serving

Directions:

1. Heat 2 teaspoons of the oil in a medium Dutch oven or flameproof casserole over medium-high heat. Add the zucchini and cook, stirring occasionally, until beginning to brown, about 3 minutes. Add the onion and garlic and cook, stirring occasionally, until the onions soften, about 2 minutes. Stir in the tomatoes and cook just until they are warm, about 1 minute. Season with the salt and pepper. Transfer to a bowl.
2. Meanwhile, bring the broth and water to a boil in a medium saucepan over high heat. Reduce the heat to very low to keep the broth mixture warm.
3. Heat the remaining 2 teaspoons oil in the Dutch oven over medium heat. Add the rice and cook, stirring well, until it turns opaque, about 2 minutes. Stir about ¾ cup of the hot broth mixture into the rice. Cook, stirring almost constantly, until the rice absorbs almost all of the broth, about 3 minutes. Add another ¾ cup of broth and stir until it is almost absorbed. Repeat, keeping the risotto at a steady simmer and adding more broth as it is absorbed, until you use all of the broth and the risotto is barely tender, about 20 minutes total. During the last minute of cooking, stir in the zucchini mixture so it can reheat. The risotto should be loose but not soupy. If you run out of stock and the risotto isn't tender, add more hot water. Stir in the oregano and lemon zest.
4. Divide evenly among four soup bowls and sprinkle each with 1 tablespoon Parmesan cheese. Serve immediately.

Nutrition Info:

- Info280 calories,10 g protein,46 g carbohydrates,7 g fat,384 mg sodiu.

Chili Stuffed Baked Potatoes

Servings: 2
Cooking Time: 45 Mins
Ingredients:

- 2 large roasting potatoes
- 1 avocado, peeled, cored, and cut into pieces
- ½ a lime, juiced
- Black pepper to taste
- ½ cup red kidney beans, drained and rinsed
- ½ cup homemade spicy tomato salsa
- ½ cup low-fat sour cream
- ¼ tsp Mexican spice blend
- ¼ cup grated gouda cheese
- 2 tsp finely chopped coriander to garnish

Directions:

1. Preheat the oven to 400ºF. Prick the potatoes with a fork and place them on the oven rack. Bake for 45 minutes until cooked all the way through.
2. In the meantime, prepare the toppings. Smash the avocado and lime juice together in a small bowl and set aside.
3. Mix sour cream and Mexican spice and then mix the beans and salsa in a separate bowl.
4. Once the potatoes are cooked, cut them down the middle and stuff the bean mixture into them. Spoon the avocado onto them and top with sour cream mixture and grated cheese.
5. Serve hot, garnished with coriander, and enjoy.

Nutrition Info:

- Info624 calories,91g carbs,24g protein,366mg sodium,21g fat.

Chilled Cucumber-and-avocado Soup With Dill

Servings:4
Cooking Time:x
Ingredients:

- 2 English cucumbers, peeled and diced, plus ¼ cup reserved for garnish
- 1 avocado, peeled, pitted, and diced, plus ¼ cup reserved for garnish
- 1½ cups nonfat or low-fat plain Greek yogurt
- ½ cup cold water
- ⅓ cup loosely packed dill, plus sprigs for garnish
- 1 tablespoon freshly squeezed lemon juice
- ¼ teaspoon freshly ground black pepper
- ¼ teaspoon salt
- 1 clove garlic

Directions:

1. Purée ingredients in a blender until smooth. If you prefer a thinner soup, add more water until you reach the desired consistency.
2. Divide soup among 4 bowls. Cover with plastic wrap and refrigerate for 30 minutes.
3. Garnish with cucumber, avocado, and dill sprigs, if desired.

Nutrition Info:

- InfoCalories: 142,Total Fat: 7g,Sodium: 193mg,Total Carbohydrate: 12g,Protein: 11.

Spinach Burgers

Servings:4
Cooking Time:x
Ingredients:

- 1 teaspoon olive oil
- 1 medium red onion, peeled and diced
- 4 cloves garlic, peeled and minced
- 1 medium red bell pepper, seeded and diced
- 6 cups baby spinach
- 1 ½ teaspoons salt-free Italian seasoning
- ½ teaspoon ground black pepper
- 1 large egg white
- ¼ cup shredded Swiss cheese
- ½ cup salt-free bread crumbs

Directions:

1. Preheat oven to 425°F. Spray a baking sheet lightly with nonstick cooking spray and set aside.
2. Heat oil in a large skillet over medium heat. Add onion and garlic and sauté for 2 minutes. Add bell pepper and sauté for 2 minutes. Add spinach and sauté until wilted, about 2 minutes more. Remove skillet from heat.
3. Add Italian seasoning and black pepper and stir, scraping up the brown bits from the bottom of the skillet. Set aside to cool for 5 minutes.
4. Add egg white, cheese, and bread crumbs to skillet and stir to combine. Form mixture into 4 patties.
5. Place patties on prepared baking sheet. Place sheet on middle rack in oven and bake for 10 minutes. Flip patties and bake for another 5 minutes.
6. Remove from oven and serve immediately.

Nutrition Info:

- InfoCalories 111,Fat 3g,Sodium 66mg,Carbohydrates 15g,Protein 6g

Quinoa And Red Lentil Stuffed Peppers With A Creamy Cashew Sauce

Servings:4
Cooking Time:1 Hour 10 Minutes
Ingredients:

- ½ cup quinoa, rinsed
- ½ cup red lentils (see Tip), rinsed
- ½ cup raw cashews
- ¼ cup fresh lemon juice
- 3 to 4 teaspoons minced garlic
- 1 cup fresh basil leaves
- Pinch of salt
- ¼ teaspoon freshly ground black pepper
- 1 cup riced cauliflower (see Tip, this page)
- 2 cups baby spinach or baby kale, chopped
- ¼ cup nutritional yeast
- 2 teaspoons dried thyme
- Pinch of cayenne pepper
- 4 large bell peppers, any color, halved lengthwise
- Fresh chives (optional)

Directions:

1. In a saucepan, combine the quinoa, lentils, and 2 cups water and bring to a boil over high heat. Reduce the heat, cover, and simmer until the liquid is absorbed, the quinoa is fluffy, and the lentils are tender, 15 to 20 minutes.
2. Preheat the oven to 375°F. Pour ½ inch water into a baking dish big enough to hold the pepper halves in a single layer.
3. Meanwhile, in a food processor or high-powered blender, combine the cashews, ½ cup water, the lemon juice, garlic to taste, basil, salt, and black pepper and process until creamy and smooth. Pour into a medium bowl.
4. To the bowl, add the cooked quinoa and lentils, riced cauliflower, spinach, nutritional yeast, thyme, and cayenne. Mix thoroughly to combine.
5. Lightly spray the halved peppers with nonstick cooking spray and place cut side up in the baking dish. Dividing evenly, spoon the filling into each bell pepper cavity until full. Cover with foil and bake for 30 minutes. Remove the foil and bake until the peppers are soft and slightly golden brown, another 15 to 20 minutes.
6. Garnish with fresh chives, if desired, and serve immediately.

Nutrition Info:

- InfoCalories 326,Sodium 73 mg,Total carbohydrates 47 g,Protein 17 .

Coconut Rice And White Beans

Servings:2
Cooking Time:30 Minutes
Ingredients:

- 1 stalk lemongrass, bottom 6 inches only, outer leaves peeled
- 1 teaspoon extra-virgin olive oil
- 2 cloves garlic, minced
- 2 tablespoons minced shallot
- ½ cup chopped red bell pepper
- 1 cup cubed and peeled eggplant
- 1 teaspoon ground cardamom
- 1 teaspoon ground coriander
- ½ teaspoon ground cinnamon
- ½ cup canned no-salt-added diced tomatoes and their juices
- ½ cup black rice (see Tip)
- ⅔ cup canned "lite" coconut milk
- 1 can small white beans, rinsed and drained
- 2 cups chopped baby kale
- ½ lime
- Hot sauce (optional)
- Salt and freshly ground black pepper (optional)

Directions:

1. Lightly pound the lemongrass stalk with a kitchen mallet.
2. In a large pot, heat the olive oil over high heat. Add the garlic and shallot and cook until soft, 3 to 5 minutes. Add the bell pepper and eggplant and continue cooking until softened, 3 to 5 minutes.
3. Add the cardamom, coriander, and cinnamon and cook for 1 more minute, stirring occasionally to prevent the spices from burning.
4. Add the tomatoes, black rice, coconut milk, 1½ cups water, and beans and stir to combine. Cover, bring to a boil, then reduce the heat to low and allow to simmer for 20 minutes.
5. Stir in the kale, cover, and continue cooking until the kale is wilted, the rice is done, and most of the liquid is absorbed, 5 to 8 minutes longer.
6. To serve, remove the lemongrass stalk and squeeze in the lime juice. If desired, season with hot sauce and a dash of salt and black pepper.

Nutrition Info:

- InfoCalories 433,Sodium 32 mg,Total carbohydrates 75 g,Protein 19 .

Amazing Veggie Casserole

Servings:8
Cooking Time: 25 Minutes
Ingredients:

- 2 teaspoons olive oil
- 2 medium onions, sliced thinly
- 1/2 medium head green cabbage, sliced
- 1 pound kale, leaves only, chopped
- 3 medium carrots, sliced into thin sticks
- 1/2 cup low-sodium vegetable broth or water
- 2 tablespoons low-sodium soy sauce
- TOPPING
- 1 1/2 cups salt-free bread crumbs
- 8 ounces extra-firm tofu
- 1/4 cup chopped walnuts
- 2 garlic cloves
- 2 tablespoons olive oil
- 2 teaspoons dried basil
- 1 1/2 teaspoons dried oregano
- 1 teaspoon ground sweet paprika

Directions:
1. Preheat oven to 350°F. Take out a 9" × 13" baking dish and set aside.
2. Heat olive oil in a large sauté pan over medium heat. Add onion, cabbage, kale, carrots, broth, and soy sauce. Cover the pan and cook, stirring occasionally, for 10 minutes. Transfer contents to the baking pan and set aside.
3. To make the topping, measure remaining ingredients into a food processor and pulse to combine. Sprinkle over vegetables in baking dish.
4. Place dish on middle rack in oven and bake, uncovered, until topping is golden brown and vegetables are heated through, about 15 minutes.
5. Remove from oven and serve immediately.

Nutrition Info:
- InfoCalories: 238,Fat: 9 g,Protein: 10 g,Sodium: 69 ml,Carbohydrates: 33 .

Crustless Vegan Mushroom And Sweet Potato Mini Quiches

Servings:2
Cooking Time:35 Minutes
Ingredients:

- 1 cup chickpea flour
- 1/4 cup nutritional yeast
- 1 teaspoon baking powder
- 2 teaspoons ground sage
- 1 teaspoon dried thyme
- 1 teaspoon ground turmeric
- Pinch of salt (black salt, if possible; see Tip)
- Freshly ground black pepper
- 1 cup unsweetened cashew milk (or fat-free dairy milk if you are not vegan)
- 2/3 cup frozen green peas, slightly thawed
- 1 cup riced cauliflower and sweet potato (see Tip)
- 1 cup finely chopped button mushrooms
- 1 teaspoon minced garlic
- 1 tablespoon minced shallot

Directions:
1. Preheat the oven to 375°F. For a main course, lightly coat four 1-cup ramekins with cooking spray; for a snack or side, spray 8 cups of a muffin tin.
2. In a medium bowl, stir together the chickpea flour, nutritional yeast, baking powder, sage, thyme, turmeric, salt, and black pepper to taste. Stir in the milk.
3. Add the peas, riced cauliflower and sweet potato, mushrooms, garlic, and shallot and mix to combine. The batter will be thin.
4. Divide the batter evenly among the prepared ramekins or muffin cups. Transfer to the oven and bake until firm to the touch and lightly browned, about 35 minutes.
5. Remove from the oven and let sit for an additional 10 minutes (they will continue to firm up), then transfer to a wire rack and allow to cool slightly if eating immediately or completely if storing for later. Store in an airtight container in the refrigerator for up to 1 week.

Nutrition Info:
- InfoCalories 178,Sodium 89 mg,Total carbohydrates 29 g,Protein 12 .

Speedy Samosa Pasta

Servings:6
Cooking Time: 15 Minutes
Ingredients:

- 12 ounces whole-grain angel hair pasta
- 2 cups frozen peas
- 2 medium potatoes
- 1 medium onion
- 2 cloves garlic, minced
- 3 tablespoons unsalted butter or olive oil
- ¼ cup nutritional yeast flakes
- 1 tablespoon salt-free curry powder
- Freshly ground black pepper, to taste

Directions:

1. Cook pasta according to package directions, omitting salt.
2. When there are a few minutes left for the pasta to cook, add the frozen peas to the pot and return to boiling. Once cooked, drain, and return pasta and peas to the pot.
3. While the pasta is cooking, scrub the potatoes and pierce with the tines of a fork. Place potatoes in the microwave and cook roughly 8 minutes, turning once. Once cooked, remove potatoes from microwave, let rest briefly to cool, then dice.
4. While the pasta and potatoes are cooking, heat a small nonstick skillet over medium heat. Add the onion and garlic and cook, stirring, 5 minutes.
5. Add the diced potatoes, onion, and garlic to the pasta and peas. Add the butter (or olive oil) and season with the remaining ingredients. Toss well to coat.
6. Serve immediately.

Nutrition Info:

- InfoCalories: 347,Fat: 7 g,Protein: 13 g,Sodium: 46 ml,Carbohydrates: 60 .

Butternut-squash Macaroni And Cheese

Servings:2
Cooking Time: 20 Minutes
Ingredients:

- 1 cup whole-wheat ziti macaroni
- 2 cups peeled and cubed butternut squash
- 1 cup nonfat or low-fat milk, divided
- Freshly ground black pepper
- 1 teaspoon Dijon mustard
- 1 tablespoon olive oil
- ¼ cup shredded low-fat cheddar cheese

Directions:

1. Cook the pasta al dente.
2. In a medium saucepan, add the butternut squash and ½ cup milk, and place over medium-high heat. Season with black pepper. Bring to a simmer. Reduce heat to low, cover, and cook until fork tender, 8 to 10 minutes.
3. To a blender, add squash and Dijon mustard. Purée until smooth.
4. Meanwhile, place a large sauté pan over medium heat and add olive oil. Add the squash purée and remaining ½ cup of milk. Bring to a simmer and cook until thickened, 5 minutes. Add the cheese and stir to combine.
5. Add the pasta to the sauté pan and stir to combine.
6. Serve immediately.

Nutrition Info:

- InfoCalories: 373,Total Fat: 10g,Sodium: 193mg,Total Carbohydrate: 59g,Protein: 14.

Black Bean Mushroom Burgers

Servings:: 4
Cooking Time: 20 Mins
Ingredients:
- 2 tbsp. olive oil
- ½ cup finely chopped brown mushrooms
- ¼ cup finely chopped red onion
- 1 tsp ground cumin
- Black pepper to taste
- 1 tsp barbeque spice
- 1 tsp smoked paprika
- ½ tsp finely chopped fresh thyme
- ½ tsp finely chopped fresh parsley
- 15 ounces black beans, cooked and drained
- ½ cup rolled oats
- 4 burger buns

Directions:
1. Heat 1 tbsp. olive oil in a pan, add in the mushrooms and onion and fry until the mushrooms have released all their juices and the onion is translucent for about 4 minutes.
2. Add in the cumin, pepper, barbeque spice, paprika, and fresh herbs, and fry for 1 minute. Then add the black beans and cook for 3 minutes.
3. Remove from the heat, let cool slightly, and mix in the oats. Mix to form a firm burger mixture. Shape 4 burgers from this mixture. Let rest in the fridge for 5 minutes.
4. Heat the remaining oil in a clean pan, and then fry the burger patties for about 4-5 minutes per side, or until a crisp outer layer forms.
5. Serve hot with the buns.

Nutrition Info:
- Info368 calories,66g carbs,13g protein,322mg sodium,6g fat.

Linguine With Plum Tomatoes, Mushrooms, And Tempeh

Servings:6
Cooking Time:x
Ingredients:
- 1 pound dry whole-grain linguine
- 1 can no-salt-added plum tomatoes
- 1 tablespoon olive oil
- 1 large onion, diced
- 8 ounces fresh mushrooms, sliced
- 1 package organic tempeh, diced
- 3 cloves garlic, minced
- 1 teaspoon dried Italian seasoning
- 1⁄2 teaspoon freshly ground black pepper
- 1⁄8 teaspoon dried red pepper flakes

Directions:
1. Cook linguine according to package directions, omitting salt. Drain and set aside.
2. Chop the tomatoes and set aside with reserved juice from can.
3. Heat oil in a sauté pan over medium heat. Add the onion, mushrooms, tempeh, and garlic and cook, stirring, for 5 minutes.
4. Add the tomatoes with juice and seasonings. Cook, stirring occasionally, for 10 minutes.
5. Spoon sauce over pasta and serve immediately.

Nutrition Info:
- InfoCalories: 358,Fat: 8 g,Protein: 19 g,Sodium: 27 mg,Carbohydrates: 60 .

Quinoa With Mixed Vegetables And Cilantro Peanut Pesto

Servings:6
Cooking Time:x
Ingredients:

- 1 cup quinoa
- 2 cups water
- 1 teaspoon olive oil
- 1 medium red onion, peeled and diced
- 2 medium carrots, peeled and diced
- 8 ounces mushrooms, chopped
- 1 medium red bell pepper, seeded and diced
- 3 tablespoons Cilantro Peanut Pesto
- 2 scallions, sliced
- ¼ teaspoon ground black pepper

Directions:

1. Measure quinoa into a small saucepan. Add water and bring to a boil over high heat. Reduce heat to medium-low, cover, and simmer for 15 minutes.
2. Heat oil in a medium skillet over medium heat. Add onion and sauté for 2 minutes.
3. Add carrots, mushrooms, and bell pepper and cook, stirring, for 8 minutes. Remove from heat.
4. Stir in quinoa and pesto. Sprinkle with scallions and black pepper. Serve immediately.

Nutrition Info:

- InfoCalories 204,Fat 4g,Sodium 59mg,Carbohydrates 35g,Protein 7g

North-african Garbanzo Bean Tagine

Servings: 2-3
Cooking Time: 45 Mins
Ingredients:

- ½ cup minced red onion
- 1 cup carrots, diced
- 1 orange flesh sweet potato, cut into small cubes
- 2 tsp olive oil
- ¼ tsp cinnamon
- 2 cinnamon sticks
- ½ tsp cumin
- 1 tsp curry powder
- ½ tsp smoked paprika
- ½ tsp turmeric
- 1 tbsp. tomato paste
- 1 cup low sodium vegetable stock
- 1 ½ cups fresh yellow paprika peppers, diced
- 1 tbsp. minced garlic
- 1 cup cherry tomatoes, diced
- 15 ounces cooked garbanzo beans, rinsed and drained
- ½ cup dates pitted and finely chopped

Directions:

1. To start, fry the onion, carrots, and sweet potato in the olive oil, in a medium pot, for about 4 minutes.
2. Then add the cinnamon sticks, cinnamon, cumin, curry powder, smoked paprika, and turmeric. Fry for 1 minute, then add in the tomato paste. Fry for a further minute, and pour in the veg stock. Bring to a low simmer.
3. Add in the fresh paprika, garlic, and tomatoes and cook for 5 minutes.
4. Add the garbanzo beans and dates and simmer, covered for about 30 minutes. The vegetable should all be cooked through and the tagine lovely and aromatic.
5. Serve hot and enjoy.

Nutrition Info:

- Info469 calories,88g carbs,16g protein,256mg sodium,9g fat.

Pasta With Tomatoes And Peas

Servings:2
Cooking Time: 15 Minutes
Ingredients:

- ½ cup whole-grain pasta of choice
- 8 cups water, plus ¼ for finishing
- 1 cup frozen peas
- 1 tablespoon olive oil
- 1 cup cherry tomatoes, halved
- ¼ teaspoon freshly ground black pepper
- 1 teaspoon dried basil
- ¼ cup grated Parmesan cheese (low-sodium)

Directions:

1. Cook the pasta al dente.
2. Add the water to the same pot you used to cook the pasta, and when it's boiling add the peas. Cook until tender but still firm, about 5 minutes. Drain and set aside.
3. Heat the oil in a large skillet over medium heat. Add the cherry tomatoes, put a lid on the skillet and let the tomatoes soften for about 5 minutes, stirring a few times.
4. Season with black pepper and basil.
5. Toss in the pasta, peas, and ¼ cup of water, stir and remove from the heat.
6. Serve topped with Parmesan.

Nutrition Info:

- InfoCalories: 266,Total Fat: 12g,Sodium: 320mg,Total Carbohydrate: 30g,Protein: 13.

Black-eyed Peas And Greens Power Salad

Servings:2
Cooking Time: 6 Minutes
Ingredients:

- 1 tablespoon olive oil
- 3 cups purple cabbage, chopped
- 5 cups baby spinach
- 1 cup shredded carrots
- 1 can black-eyed peas, drained and rinsed
- Juice of ½ lemon
- Salt
- Freshly ground black pepper

Directions:

1. In a medium pan, add the oil and cabbage and sauté for 1 to 2 minutes on medium heat.
2. Next add in your spinach, cover for 3 to 4 minutes on medium heat, until greens are wilted.
3. Remove from the heat and add to a large bowl.
4. Add in the carrots, black-eyed peas, and a splash of lemon juice.
5. Season with salt and pepper, if desired.
6. Toss together and serve.

Nutrition Info:

- InfoCalories: 320,Total Fat: 9g,Sodium: 351mg,Total Carbohydrate: 49g,Protein: 16.

Salads And Dressings

Lentil And Goat Cheese Salad

Servings:6
Cooking Time:x
Ingredients:

- 1 cup green (Puy) or brown lentils
- 2 tablespoons sherry or cider vinegar
- 2 tablespoons water
- Freshly grated zest of 1 lemon
- ½ teaspoon kosher salt
- ¼ teaspoon freshly ground black pepper
- 2 tablespoons olive oil, preferably extra-virgin
- 1 medium red bell pepper, cored and cut into ¼-inch dice
- 2 celery ribs, cut into ¼-inch dice
- 1 medium carrot, peeled and cut into ¼-inch dice
- 2 tablespoons finely chopped fresh basil, oregano, or parsley
- 4 ounces crumbled goat cheese

Directions:
1. Bring a medium saucepan of water to a boil over high heat. Add the lentils and cook (just like pasta) until tender, about 30 minutes. Drain in a wire sieve, rinse under cold running water, and drain well.
2. In a large bowl, whisk together the vinegar, water, lemon zest, salt, and pepper. Gradually whisk in the oil.
3. Add the lentils, bell pepper, celery, carrot, and basil and toss well. Sprinkle with the goat cheese and serve chilled or at room temperature.

Nutrition Info:
- Info170 calories,9 g protein,22 g carbohydrates,5 g fat,21 mg sodium,1 fat.

Warm Potato Salad With Spinach

Servings:8
Cooking Time: 15 Minutes
Ingredients:

- 3 pounds small new potatoes or fingerlings
- 4 cups fresh baby spinach
- 5 tablespoons red wine vinegar
- 5 tablespoons olive oil
- 2 tablespoons water
- 1 tablespoon no-salt-added prepared mustard
- 1 tablespoon agave nectar
- 1 teaspoon garlic powder
- 1 teaspoon all-purpose salt-free seasoning
- 1⁄2 teaspoon dried dill
- 1⁄2 teaspoon dried Italian seasoning
- 1⁄2 teaspoon dried thyme
- Freshly ground black pepper, to taste

Directions:
1. Place unpeeled potatoes into a pot and add enough water to cover by a couple of inches. Bring to a boil over high heat. Once boiling, reduce heat to medium-high and simmer until tender, about 15 minutes.
2. Remove pot from heat and drain. Cut the potatoes into bite-sized chunks.
3. Place the potatoes back into the pot and add the spinach.
4. In a small bowl, whisk together the remaining ingredients, then pour over salad. Toss well to coat and combine.
5. Serve immediately or cover and refrigerate until ready to serve.

Nutrition Info:
- InfoCalories: 242,Fat: 9 g,Protein: 4 g,Sodium: 20 ml,Carbohydrates: 37 .

Salad Niçoise

Servings:2
Cooking Time:x
Ingredients:
- 1 small head butter lettuce
- 1 small cucumber
- 2 medium red potatoes
- 1 tablespoon white distilled vinegar
- 2 eggs
- 1 bunch fresh green beans, trimmed
- 2 tablespoons olive oil
- 2 tablespoons red wine vinegar
- 1 teaspoon salt-free prepared mustard
- 1 clove garlic, minced
- 1/2 teaspoon freshly ground black pepper
- 2 small tomatoes, quartered
- 1 can no-salt-added tuna in water, drained

Directions:
1. Wash the lettuce and pat dry. Tear the leaves into bite-sized pieces and set aside.
2. Peel the cucumber, halve lengthwise, and remove seeds using a spoon. Slice and set aside.
3. Place the potatoes into a pan and add enough water to cover. Bring to a boil over high heat, then reduce heat slightly, and simmer until tender, about 20 minutes. Once cooked, dice, toss with white vinegar, and set aside.
4. Place the eggs into a saucepan, add enough water to cover, and bring to a boil over high heat. Boil 12 minutes. Once cooked, carefully crack, peel, and slice into quarters. Set aside.
5. Bring a small pot of water to boil. Once boiling, add the green beans and cook for 2 minutes. Remove beans from pot and immediately place in a bowl of ice water. Set aside.
6. In a small bowl, add the oil, vinegar, mustard, garlic, and pepper and whisk well to combine.
7. Assemble the salad on a platter, placing lettuce on the bottom and then grouping the cucumber, potatoes, eggs, green beans, tomatoes, and tuna on top. Drizzle the dressing evenly over the salad. Serve immediately.

Nutrition Info:
- InfoCalories: 471,Fat: 20 g,Protein: 30 g,Sodium: 111 mg,Carbohydrates: 41 .

Chinese Chicken Salad

Servings:2
Cooking Time:x
Ingredients:
- 2 cups packed, shredded Napa cabbage
- 8 ounces Basic Roast Chicken Breast 101 or Classic Poached Chicken (here or here), cut into ½-inch dice
- 1 large carrot, shredded on the large holes of a box grater
- ½ medium red bell pepper, cored and cut into thin strips
- 2 tablespoons finely chopped fresh cilantro, plus more for sprinkling
- Asian Ginger Dressing (here)

Directions:
1. In a medium bowl, mix well the Napa cabbage, chicken, carrot, bell pepper, and 2 tablespoons cilantro. Stir in the dressing. Divide the salad between two bowls, sprinkle with additional cilantro, and serve chilled.

Nutrition Info:
- Info335 calories,26 g protein,14 g carbohydrates,20 g fat,760 mg sodium,3 fats.

Tarragon Chicken Salad With Grapes And Almonds

Servings:2
Cooking Time:x
Ingredients:

- 3 tablespoons plain low-fat yogurt
- 2 tablespoons light mayonnaise
- 2 teaspoons finely chopped fresh tarragon
- Pinch of kosher salt
- ¼ teaspoon freshly ground black pepper
- 8 ounces Basic Roast Chicken Breast 101 or Classic Poached Chicken (here or here), cut into ½-inch dice
- 1 cup halved red or green seedless grapes
- 2 medium celery ribs, thinly sliced
- ¼ cup sliced almonds, toasted (see "Toasting Nuts," here)
- 2 cups mixed salad greens
- Lemon wedges, for serving

Directions:

1. In a medium bowl, whisk the yogurt, mayonnaise, tarragon, salt, and pepper. Add the chicken, grapes, celery, and almonds and mix well.
2. Divide the salad greens between two salad bowls. Top each with half of the chicken mixture. Serve immediately with the lemon wedges for squeezing the juice over the salad.

Nutrition Info:

- Info352 calories,29 g protein,22 g carbohydrates,17 g fat,658 mg sodium,2 fats.

Roasted Beet Salad With Yogurt-dill Dressing

Servings:4
Cooking Time:x
Ingredients:

- 1½ pounds beets without leaves or stems, scrubbed but unpeeled
- ½ cup plain nonfat yogurt
- 1 tablespoon cider vinegar
- 1 tablespoon finely chopped fresh dill, tarragon, or parsley
- ½ teaspoon kosher salt
- ¼ teaspoon freshly ground black pepper
- 1 clove garlic, crushed through a press
- 1 cup halved grape tomatoes
- 2 scallions, white and green parts, trimmed and thinly sliced

Directions:

1. Preheat the oven to 400°F. Wrap each beet in aluminum foil.
2. Place on a rimmed baking sheet and roast until tender, about 1¼ hour, depending on the size and age of the beets. Unwrap and let cool until easy to handle. Peel the beets and cut into ½-inch-thick wedges.
3. In a medium bowl, whisk together the yogurt, vinegar, dill, salt, pepper, and garlic. Add the tomatoes, beets, and scallions and toss to coat. Cover and refrigerate until chilled, at least 1 hour and up to 12 hours. Serve chilled.

Nutrition Info:

- Info83 calories,4 g protein,17 g carbohydrates,0 g fat,325 mg sodiu.

Bean Salad With Orange Vinaigrette

Servings:6
Cooking Time:x
Ingredients:

- 1 can no-salt-added kidney beans
- 1 can no-salt-added garbanzo beans
- 1 can no-salt-added pinto beans
- 2 shallots, chopped
- 1 medium carrot, shredded
- 1 small bell pepper, diced
- 1 small stalk celery, diced
- 1/4 cup pure maple syrup
- 1/3 cup apple cider vinegar
- 2 tablespoons freshly squeezed orange juice
- 1 tablespoon olive oil
- 1 teaspoon grated orange zest
- 1/2 teaspoon freshly ground black pepper

Directions:

1. Drain and rinse all the canned beans, then place in a mixing bowl.
2. Add the chopped shallot, shredded carrot, bell pepper, and celery and stir to combine.
3. Place the remaining ingredients into a small mixing bowl and whisk well. Pour the dressing over the salad and toss to coat.
4. Serve immediately or cover and refrigerate until ready to serve.

Nutrition Info:

- InfoCalories: 393,Fat: 5 g,Protein: 19 g,Sodium: 70 mg,Carbohydrates: 69 .

Tomato Cucumber Basil Salad

Servings:4
Cooking Time:x
Ingredients:

- 2 small–medium cucumbers
- 4 ripe medium tomatoes, quartered
- 1 small onion, sliced thinly
- 1/4 cup chopped fresh basil
- 3 tablespoons red wine vinegar
- 1 tablespoon olive oil
- 1 clove garlic, minced
- 1/4 teaspoon freshly ground black pepper

Directions:

1. Peel the cucumbers. Halve lengthwise, then use a spoon to gently scrape out the seeds.
2. Slice cucumbers and place in a bowl. Add the tomatoes, onion, and basil.
3. Place the remaining ingredients into a small bowl and whisk well to combine.
4. Pour the dressing over the salad and toss to coat. Serve immediately or cover and refrigerate until ready to serve.

Nutrition Info:

- InfoCalories: 66,Fat: 4 g,Protein: 1 g,Sodium: 9 mg,Carbohydrates: 7 .

Tuna And White Bean Salad

Servings:2
Cooking Time:x
Ingredients:

- 2 tablespoons red wine vinegar
- 1 tablespoon water
- 1 small clove garlic, crushed through a press
- ¼ teaspoon dried oregano
- ¼ teaspoon kosher salt
- ¼ teaspoon crushed hot red pepper
- 1 tablespoon olive oil
- 1 can no-salt-added cannellini beans, drained and rinsed
- 1 can very low-sodium tuna in water, drained
- 1 medium red bell pepper, roasted, seeded, and diced (see "Roasting Red Peppers," opposite)
- 2 tablespoons finely chopped fresh parsley (optional)
- 2 cups mixed salad greens
- Lemon wedges, for serving

Directions:

1. In a medium bowl, whisk together the vinegar, water, garlic, oregano, salt, and hot pepper. Whisk in the oil. Add the beans, tuna, red bell pepper, and parsley (if using) and mix well. This salad can be refrigerated in a covered container for up to 2 days.
2. For each serving, put 1 cup of salad greens in a wide bowl. Top with half of the tuna and bean mixture. Serve immediately with the lemon wedges for squeezing the juice onto the salad.

Nutrition Info:

- Info402 calories,32 g protein,52 g carbohydrates,8 g fat,314 mg sodiu.

Iceberg Lettuce Wedge With Russian Dressing

Servings:2
Cooking Time:x
Ingredients:

- ½ head iceberg lettuce, cut in half lengthwise to make 2 wedges
- ½ cup halved grape tomatoes
- ½ medium cucumber, peeled and thinly sliced
- ½ small sweet onion, cut into thin half-moons
- 1 recipe Russian Dressing (here)

Directions:

1. For each serving, put an iceberg wedge on a serving plate and surround with the tomatoes, cucumber, and onion. Top each wedge with the dressing and serve.

Nutrition Info:

- Info194 calories,4 g protein,22 mg carbohydrates,11 g fat,318 mg sodium,2 fats.

Chipotle Chicken Chili Taco Salad

Servings:6
Cooking Time:x
Ingredients:

- Baked Tortilla Chips
- Olive oil in a pump sprayer
- 3 corn tortillas, cut into eighths to make 24 wedges
- Salad
- 1 tablespoon olive oil
- 1 pound boneless, skinless chicken thighs, trimmed, cut into 1-inch pieces
- 1 medium yellow onion, chopped
- 1 large red bell pepper, cored and cut into ½-inch dice
- 2 cloves garlic, minced
- 1 teaspoon dried oregano
- 1 teaspoon ground cumin
- ¼ teaspoon kosher salt
- 1 can no-salt-added diced tomatoes, drained
- ⅓ cup water
- 1 canned chipotle chili in adobo, minced
- 1 can 50 percent reduced-sodium black beans, drained and rinsed
- 1 head iceberg lettuce, cored and torn into bite-sized pieces
- 6 tablespoons low-fat sour cream, for serving
- ½ cup chopped fresh cilantro, for serving
- Lime wedges, for serving

Directions:

1. To make the tortilla chips: Preheat the oven to 400°F. Spray a rimmed baking sheet with oil. Spread the tortilla strips on the baking sheet and spray with oil. Bake, stirring occasionally, until crisp and golden brown, about 10 minutes. Let cool.
2. To make the salad: Heat 1 teaspoon of the oil in a large nonstick skillet over medium-high heat. Add the chicken and cook, stirring occasionally, until lightly browned, about 5 minutes. Transfer to a plate.
3. Heat the remaining 2 teaspoons oil in the skillet. Sauté the onion, bell pepper, and garlic, stirring occasionally, until tender, about 5 minutes. Stir in the oregano, cumin, and salt. Add the tomatoes, water, and chipotle and bring to a simmer. Return the chicken to the skillet. Reduce the heat to low, cover the skillet, and simmer until the chicken is tender and opaque throughout, about 35 minutes. During the last 5 minutes, stir in the black beans. Let cool for 10 minutes.
4. Divide the lettuce among six serving bowls and top with chili. Add 4 tortilla chips to each bowl, top with 1 tablespoon of the sour cream, and sprinkle with cilantro. Serve warm with the lime wedges.

Nutrition Info:

- Info263 calories,20 g protein,32 g carbohydrates,10 g fat,484 mg sodiu.

Creamy Low-sodium Coleslaw

Servings:6
Cooking Time:x
Ingredients:

- 1⁄2 medium head green cabbage, shredded
- 1 medium carrot, shredded
- 1 small onion, grated
- 1⁄3 cup Salt-Free Mayonnaise
- 3 tablespoons sugar
- 3 tablespoons apple cider vinegar
- 1⁄2 teaspoon dry ground mustard
- 1⁄2 teaspoon freshly ground black pepper

Directions:

1. Combine all the ingredients in a large mixing bowl and stir well.
2. Cover and refrigerate until ready to serve.

Nutrition Info:

- InfoCalories: 133,Fat: 8 g,Protein: 2 g,Sodium: 32 mg,Carbohydrates: 13 .

Roast Beef Salad With Beets, Apple, And Horseradish

Servings:4
Cooking Time:x
Ingredients:

- 4 medium beets, scrubbed but unpeeled
- 2 tablespoons cider vinegar
- 1½ tablespoons pared and freshly grated horseradish (use a zester, such as a Microplane)
- 2 tablespoons olive oil
- 1 large Rome apple, cored and cut into ½-inch dice
- 1 scallion, white and green parts, finely chopped
- 12 ounces thinly sliced Spiced Roast Eye of Round (here)

Directions:

1. Preheat the oven to 400°F. Wrap each beet in aluminum foil and place on a rimmed baking sheet. Bake until the beets are tender when pierced with the tip of a small, sharp knife, about 1¼ hours. Unwrap and let cool. Peel the beets and cut into ½-inch dice.
2. In a medium bowl, whisk together the vinegar and horseradish, then whisk in the oil. Add the beets, apple, and scallion and mix well. Cover and refrigerate until chilled, at least 1 hour or up to 1 day.
3. Divide the beet salad among four dinner plates and top with equal amounts of the sliced roast beef. Serve chilled.

Nutrition Info:

- Info285 calories,27 g protein,21 g carbohydrates,11 g fat,185 mg sodiu.

American-style French Dressing

Servings:1
Cooking Time:x
Ingredients:

- ¼ cup no-salt-added tomato ketchup
- 2 tablespoons minced shallot
- 2 tablespoons water
- 1 tablespoon cider vinegar
- 1 clove garlic, crushed through a press
- ¼ teaspoon freshly ground black pepper
- 2 tablespoons canola oil

Directions:

1. In a small bowl, whisk together the ketchup, shallot, water, vinegar, garlic, and pepper. Gradually whisk in the oil.

Nutrition Info:

- Info90 calories,0 g protein,7 g carbohydrates,7 g fat,1 mg sodium,24 mg potassium. Food groups: 1 fat.

Warm Asian Slaw

Servings:4
Cooking Time:x
Ingredients:

- 1 tablespoon sesame oil
- 1 tablespoon peanut oil
- 2 sliced scallions
- 2 cloves garlic, minced
- 1 tablespoon minced fresh ginger
- 1 medium bok choy, chopped
- 2 medium carrots, shredded
- 1 tablespoon unflavored rice vinegar
- 1/2 teaspoon sugar
- 1/2 teaspoon ground white pepper
- 1/2 tablespoon toasted sesame seeds (optional)

Directions:

1. Heat both oils in a skillet over medium. Add scallions, garlic, and ginger and cook, stirring, for 1 minute.
2. Add bok choy and carrots and sauté for 2 minutes. Remove from heat.
3. Place contents in a bowl. Stir in vinegar, sugar, and pepper. Garnish with sesame seeds, if desired.
4. Serve immediately or cover and refrigerate until ready to serve. Tastes equally great cold.

Nutrition Info:

- InfoCalories: 112,Fat: 7 g,Protein: 3 g,Sodium: 72 mg,Carbohydrates: 9 .

Shrimp, Mango, And Black Bean Salad

Servings:4
Cooking Time:x
Ingredients:

- 2 tablespoons olive oil, plus more in a pump sprayer
- ¾ pound large shrimp, peeled and deveined
- 2 tablespoons fresh lime juice
- 2 ripe mangoes, pitted, peeled, and cut into ½-inch dice (see here)
- 1 can reduced-sodium black beans, drained and rinsed
- ½ jalapeño, seeded and minced
- 2 tablespoons finely chopped fresh cilantro or mint
- 2 tablespoons minced red onion

Directions:

1. Spray a large ridged grill pan with oil and heat over medium heat. Add the shrimp to the pan. Cook, turning occasionally, until the shrimp are opaque throughout, 3 to 5 minutes. Refrigerate to cool completely, about 20 minutes.
2. In a large serving bowl, whisk together the lime juice and the 2 tablespoons oil. Add the shrimp, mango, beans, jalapeño, cilantro, and onion and toss gently. Serve immediately.

Nutrition Info:

- Info213 calories,18 g protein,36 g carbohydrates,2 g fat,679 mg sodium,1 fat.

Kale, Pear, And Bulgur Salad

Servings:4
Cooking Time:x
Ingredients:

- ½ cup bulgur
- 1¾ cups boiling water
- 8 ounces curly kale
- 2 tablespoons fresh lemon juice
- ½ teaspoon kosher salt
- 2 ripe pears, such as Anjou or Comice, cored and thinly sliced
- ½ cup walnut pieces, toasted (see "Toasting Nuts," here) and coarsely chopped
- 2 tablespoons extra-virgin olive oil
- Freshly ground black pepper

Directions:

1. Put the bulgur in a medium heatproof bowl and add the boiling water. Let stand until the bulgur is tender, about 30 minutes. Drain in a wire sieve. Press the excess liquid from the bulgur. Set aside.
2. Pull off and discard the thick stems from the kale. Taking a few pieces at a time, stack the kale and coarsely slice crosswise into ½-inch-thick strips. Transfer to a large bowl of cold water and agitate to loosen any grit. Lift the kale out of the water, leaving any dirt behind in the water. Dry the kale in a salad spinner or pat dry with paper towels.
3. Sprinkle the kale with the lemon juice and salt. Using your hands, rub the kale until softened, about 2 minutes. Fluff the bulgur with a fork and add to the kale with the pears and walnuts. Drizzle with the oil and toss. Season with the pepper. Serve at once or refrigerate for up to 2 hours.

Nutrition Info:

- Info295 calories,8 g protein,34 g carbohydrates,17 g fat,278 mg sodium,1 fat.

Asian Shrimp Salad

Servings: 2
Cooking Time: 3 Mins
Ingredients:

- 2 tbsp. minced fresh ginger
- 1tsp low sodium soy sauce
- ¼ tsp ground dried chili
- 1 tbsp. grapeseed oil
- ½ tsp sesame seed oil
- 2 tbsp. apple cider vinegar
- 8-ounces shrimp, cooked, deveined, peeled, and cubed
- 1 cup coarsely grated carrots
- ¼ roasted, chopped cashew nuts - unsalted
- 1 medium sweet red pepper, sliced
- 2 tbsp. diced spring onions
- 1 cup fresh snow peas, topped and tailed and halved
- 6 cups mixed baby Asian greens

Directions:

1. In a glass measuring jug, mix the salad dressing Ingredients: ginger, soy sauce, chili, grapeseed oil, sesame oil, and apple cider vinegar. Whisk lightly to combine. Set aside.
2. Place the shrimp, carrots, nuts, peppers, and spring onion in a bowl.
3. Bring a small pot of water to a boil and lightly blanch the snow peas for 1-2 minutes. They should remain a vibrant green color and retain some of their crunch. Run under cold water to cool them and prevent them from cooking any further.
4. Once cooled, add the peas to the bowl with the shrimps and vegetables in, and pour over the dressing. Stir gently with a spoon.
5. Place half the Asian greens onto each plate and divide the shrimp mixture between the two. Place the shrimp in the center of your greens and serve immediately.
6. Enjoy!

Nutrition Info:

- Info403 calories,23g carbs,32g protein,568mg sodium,18g fat.

Weeknight Tossed Green Salad

Servings:4
Cooking Time:x
Ingredients:

- 1 mixed salad greens
- 1 cup halved grape tomatoes
- 1 cucumber, peeled, seeded, and sliced
- ½ cup sunflower or pumpkin seeds or sliced natural almonds
- American-Style French Dressing, Lemon Vinaigrette, Mustard Vinaigrette, Creamy Ranch Dressing, or Russian Dressing (here)

Directions:

1. Toss the salad greens, tomatoes, and cucumber together in a large bowl. Sprinkle with the seeds. Drizzle with the dressing and toss again. Serve immediately.

Nutrition Info:

- Info89 calories,4 g protein,7 g carbohydrates,6 g fat,10 mg sodiu.

Tomato Garlic Dressing

Servings:1
Cooking Time:x
Ingredients:

- 2 tablespoons red wine vinegar
- 2 tablespoons lemon juice
- 1 tablespoon salt-free tomato paste
- 1½ teaspoons olive oil
- 2 cloves garlic
- 1 teaspoon agave nectar
- 1/8 teaspoon ground white pepper

Directions:

1. Place all of the ingredients into a food processor and pulse until smooth.
2. Serve immediately or store in an airtight container until ready to serve.

Nutrition Info:

- InfoCalories: 60,Fat: 2 g,Protein: 0 g,Sodium: 7 mg,Carbohydrates: 9 .

Soups, Stews, And Chilis

New York Chowder

Servings: 8
Cooking Time: 35 Mins
Ingredients:

- 1 tbsp. canola oil
- 1 red onion, diced
- 2 large waxy potatoes, washed and cut into small dices
- 2 medium parsnips, peeled and diced
- 2 celery stalks, cut into dice
- Black pepper to taste
- 1 tsp fresh, finely chopped basil, plus extra sprigs to serve
- ½ tsp fresh finely chopped oregano
- 1 bay leaf
- 5 cups low sodium fish stock
- 2 cups water
- 2 14.5-ounce cans chopped tomatoes
- 16 ounces grouper filets, skin removed, cut into pieces
- Finely chopped parsley to garnish

Directions:

1. In a large pot, heat the oil, then add in the onion, potatoes, parsnips, celery, and black pepper. Fry until the onions are translucent, about 5 minutes.
2. Add in the basil and oregano and stir for 1 minute. Then pour in the stock and water and add the bay leaf.
3. Bring to a steady boil and cook for 15 minutes, or until the potatoes are soft. Add in the tomatoes, and cook, uncovered, for a further 10 minutes to combine the flavors.
4. Lastly, add in the fish pieces and cook until white and flaky, about 3 minutes.
5. Remove the bay leaf and discard.
6. Serve hot, with a sprinkling of parsley to garnish.

Nutrition Info:

- Info143 calories,17g carbs,14g protein,714mg sodium,2g fat.

Barley Soup With Asparagus And Mushrooms

Servings:4
Cooking Time:1 Hour
Ingredients:

- 2 tablespoons extra-virgin olive oil
- 1 clove garlic, minced
- 1 medium onion, chopped
- 1 medium carrot, diced
- 1 small bunch asparagus, tough ends trimmed, cut into 1- to 2-inch pieces
- 10 ounces mushrooms, sliced
- ¾ cup pearl barley (or hulled barley, soaked overnight)
- 4 cups low-sodium vegetable broth
- 2 bay leaves
- 1 teaspoon dried marjoram
- 1 teaspoon sweet paprika
- ½ teaspoon ground turmeric
- 1 can white beans, rinsed and drained
- 4 leaves kale, midribs removed, thinly sliced
- 3 tablespoons cooking sherry
- Freshly ground black pepper (optional)
- ¼ cup minced fresh parsley

Directions:

1. In a large soup pot, heat the olive oil over medium heat. Add the garlic, onion, and carrot and cook, stirring occasionally, until the vegetables have softened, 8 to 10 minutes.
2. Add the asparagus and mushrooms, stir well, and continue to cook for another 5 minutes.
3. Add the barley, broth, bay leaves, marjoram, paprika, and turmeric and bring to a boil. Reduce the heat to low, cover, and simmer until the barley is tender and plumps up, 30 to 40 minutes for pearl barley, 60 minutes for hulled barley. If the soup seems too thick at any point, add more water, ½ cup at a time.
4. When the barley is tender, stir in the beans, kale, and sherry and continue to cook for 10 minutes.
5. Season with pepper, if desired, and stir in the parsley before serving.

Nutrition Info:

- InfoCalories 372,Sodium 173 mg,Total carbohydrates 69 g,Protein 14 .

Warming Meaty Soup

Servings: 8
Cooking Time: 30 Mins
Ingredients:
- 1 tbsp. olive oil
- 24 ounces ground beef chuck
- 2 cups diced red onion
- 2 sweet carrots, diced
- 2 stalks celery, diced
- 2 medium celeriac roots, diced
- 1 tbsp. fresh finely chopped thyme
- 2 cups uncooked barley
- 5 cups low sodium beef stock
- 2 cups water
- 1 14.5-ounce can chopped tomatoes
- Black pepper to taste
- 1 bay leaf

Directions:
1. Heat the oil in a large pot, add the ground beef and cook for about 5 minutes.
2. Add the onion, carrots, celery, celeriac, and thyme to the pot and fry for a further 5 minutes until the onion is soft.
3. Add in the barley and stir to mix well.
4. Pour in the stock, water, and chopped tomatoes. Add the bay leaf and season to taste with black pepper.
5. Bring to a boil and cook for about 20 minutes, until the barley and vegetables are soft.
6. Serve hot and enjoy.

Nutrition Info:
- Info272 calories,28g carbs,24g protein,395mg sodium,7g fat.

Hearty Vegetable Beef Soup

Servings:8
Cooking Time:x
Ingredients:
- 1 pound lean ground beef
- 1 large onion, diced
- 3 medium carrots, sliced
- 3 medium stalks celery, sliced
- 6 cloves garlic, minced
- 1 can no-salt-added diced tomatoes
- 1 can no-salt-added tomato sauce
- 4 cups low-sodium beef broth
- 2 teaspoons dried Italian seasoning
- Freshly ground black pepper, to taste

Directions:
1. Brown ground beef in a stockpot over medium heat. Once beef is cooked, carefully drain out any excess fat.
2. Add remaining ingredients to the pot, raise heat to high, and bring to a boil.
3. Once boiling, reduce heat to low, cover, and simmer for 25–30 minutes, stirring occasionally.
4. Remove from heat and serve immediately.

Nutrition Info:
- InfoCalories: 121,Fat: 3 g,Protein: 13 g,Sodium: 85 mg,Carbohydrates: 11 .

Sweet Potato, Collard, And Black-eyed Pea Soup

Servings:8
Cooking Time:x
Ingredients:

- 1 tablespoon canola oil
- 1 ham steak, cut into bite-sized pieces
- 1 large yellow onion, chopped
- 2 cloves garlic, minced
- 1 quart Homemade Chicken Broth (here)
- 3 cups water
- 1 pound sweet potatoes (yams), peeled and cut into ½-inch dice
- ½ teaspoon salt
- ½ teaspoon crushed hot red pepper
- 4 packed cups thinly sliced collard greens (wash well and remove thick stems before slicing)
- 1 cup frozen black-eyed peas

Directions:

1. Heat the oil in a large pot over medium heat. Add the ham and cook, stirring occasionally, until lightly browned, about 3 minutes. Add the onion and garlic and cook, stirring, until the onion softens, about 5 minutes.
2. Add the broth, water, sweet potatoes, salt, and hot pepper and bring to a boil over high heat. Return the heat to medium and cook at a low boil until the sweet potatoes begin to soften, about 10 minutes. Stir in the collards and black-eyed peas and cook until the greens and sweet potatoes are tender, about 10 minutes longer. Ladle into soup bowls and serve hot.

Nutrition Info:

- Info172 calories,11 g protein,24 g carbohydrates,4 g fat,547 mg sodiu.

Two-bean Tempeh Chili

Servings:8
Cooking Time:x
Ingredients:

- 1 can no-salt-added kidney beans
- 1 can no-salt-added pinto beans
- 1 package organic tempeh, cubed
- 1 medium onion, diced
- 3 cloves garlic, minced
- 2 cans no-salt-added diced tomatoes
- 2 medium carrots, diced
- 1 medium bell pepper, diced
- 1 jalapeño pepper, minced
- 1 can salt-free tomato paste
- 3 cans no-salt-added tomato sauce
- 2 teaspoons salt-free chili seasoning
- 1 teaspoon sugar
- 1¾ cups frozen corn kernels
- ¼ cup chopped fresh cilantro
- Freshly ground black pepper, to taste

Directions:

1. Drain and rinse the beans. Set aside.
2. Place a stockpot over medium heat. Add the cubed tempeh, onion, and garlic and sauté for 3 minutes.
3. Add the diced tomatoes, carrot, bell pepper, and jalapeño and sauté for 5 minutes.
4. Stir in the tomato paste, then add the tomato sauce, beans, chili seasoning, and sugar. Stir well to combine. Bring to a boil.
5. Once boiling, reduce heat to low, cover, and simmer for 20 minutes, stirring occasionally.
6. Stir in the corn kernels and simmer just until heated through.
7. Remove pot from heat. Stir in the cilantro and season to taste with black pepper. Serve immediately.

Nutrition Info:

- InfoCalories: 326,Fat: 4 g,Protein: 19 g,Sodium: 97 mg,Carbohydrates: 58 .

Garden Tomato Soup

Servings:4
Cooking Time:x
Ingredients:

- 1 tablespoon olive oil
- 3 cups chopped, peeled, and seeded tomatoes
- 1 cup chopped onion
- 1 cup chopped red bell pepper
- 1 tablespoon minced garlic
- 4 cups low-sodium vegetable broth
- 2 tablespoons no-salt-added tomato paste
- 1 tablespoon chopped fresh basil
- 1 teaspoon chopped fresh oregano
- 1/2 teaspoon chopped fresh thyme
- Freshly ground black pepper, to taste

Directions:

1. Heat the oil in a stockpot over medium heat. Add the tomatoes, onion, bell pepper, and garlic and cook, stirring, for 10 minutes.
2. Add the remaining ingredients and stir to combine. Raise heat to high and bring to a boil.
3. Once boiling, reduce heat to low, cover, and simmer for 10 minutes.
4. Remove from heat and purée using a blender or food processor. Serve immediately.

Nutrition Info:

- InfoCalories: 130,Fat: 5 g,Protein: 3 g,Sodium: 20 mg,Carbohydrates: 19 .

New England Clam Chowder

Servings: 8
Cooking Time: 35 Mins
Ingredients:

- 1/2 cup pancetta, cut into cubes
- 1 tsp olive oil
- 8 ounces potato, washed and diced
- 2 1/4 cups water
- 1 tbsp. unsalted butter
- 2 shallots, diced
- 1/2 tsp fresh thyme, finely chopped, extra sprigs to serve
- Black pepper to taste
- 1 3/4 cups low sodium chicken stock
- 2 cups low fat milk
- 2 tbsp. corn flour
- 1 cup clams, chopped, with juices

Directions:

1. Heat the olive oil in a large pot and fry the pancetta cubes until crispy and brown, about 5 minutes. Set aside to cool.
2. Meanwhile, bring 2 cups of water to a boil in a separate pot, and boil the potato until cooked, about 15 minutes.
3. Add the butter to the pancetta pot, turn the heat back on, and add the shallots, thyme, and black pepper. Fry until the shallots are translucent, about 3 minutes.
4. Add the pancetta back into the pot along with the potatoes and their water, the stock, and the milk. Bring to a boil and then cook on medium heat for 10 minutes.
5. Whisk the corn flour into the remaining 1/4 cup water, and then add it into the soup. Whisk well to prevent lumps forming.
6. Add in the clams and their juices, bring back to a boil and remove from heat.
7. Serve hot with a sprig of thyme to garnish.

Nutrition Info:

- Info120 calories,12g carbs,9g protein,424mg sodium,4g fat.

Black Bean Vegetable Soup

Servings:4
Cooking Time:x
Ingredients:

- 2½ cups low-sodium vegetable broth
- 1 small red onion, diced
- 3 cloves garlic, minced
- 1 small carrot, diced
- 1 small stalk celery, diced
- 1 small sweet potato, diced
- 1 can no-salt-added diced tomatoes
- 1 can no-salt-added black beans
- ¼ cup red wine
- 1 tablespoon no-salt-added tomato paste
- 1½ teaspoons ground cumin
- 1 teaspoon dried oregano
- ½ teaspoon ground coriander
- ¼ teaspoon dried red pepper flakes
- Freshly ground black pepper, to taste
- 2 tablespoons chopped fresh cilantro

Directions:
1. Place a stockpot over medium heat. Add ¼ cup of the vegetable broth, onion, and garlic and sauté for 2 minutes.
2. Add another ¼ cup broth, carrot, celery, sweet potato, and tomatoes with juice and sauté for 3 minutes.
3. Add remaining ingredients, except cilantro. Bring to a boil, cover, and simmer for 15–20 minutes, until veggies are tender.
4. Remove from heat, stir in the cilantro, and serve immediately.

Nutrition Info:
- InfoCalories: 233,Fat: 2 g,Protein: 10 g,Sodium: 88 mg,Carbohydrates: 41 .

Homemade Clam Chowder

Servings:8
Cooking Time:x
Ingredients:

- 1 large red-skinned potato, scrubbed but unpeeled, cut into ½-inch cubes
- 2¼ cups water, divided
- 1 teaspoon canola oil
- 2 strips reduced-sodium bacon, cut into 1-inch pieces
- 1 tablespoon unsalted butter
- 1 medium onion, chopped
- 1¾ cups Homemade Chicken Broth (here), or 1 can low-sodium chicken broth
- 2 cups low-fat milk
- ¼ teaspoon dried thyme
- ¼ teaspoon freshly ground black pepper
- 2 tablespoons cornstarch
- 1 cup chopped clams with juice

Directions:
1. Bring the potatoes and 2 cups of the water to a boil in a medium saucepan. Reduce the heat and simmer until the potatoes are barely tender, about 15 minutes.
2. Meanwhile, heat the oil in a large saucepan over medium heat. Add the bacon and cook, flipping the bacon occasionally, until browned, about 5 minutes. Transfer to a cutting board, let cool, and coarsely chop the bacon.
3. Melt the butter in the large saucepan over medium heat, add the onion, and sauté, stirring occasionally, until softened, about 3 minutes. Return the bacon to the saucepan along with the potatoes and their water, the broth, milk, thyme, and pepper. Bring to a simmer and cook over medium-low heat to blend the flavors, about 10 minutes.
4. In a small bowl, sprinkle the cornstarch over the remaining ¼ cup water, stir until dissolved, and whisk into the simmering soup. Add the clams and their juice and bring just to a boil. Serve hot.

Nutrition Info:
- Info120 calories,9 g protein,12 g carbohydrates,4 g fat,424 mg sodium,1 fa.

Pumpkin And Coconut Soup

Servings: 2
Cooking Time: 15 Mins
Ingredients:

- 2 tbsp. Coconut oil
- 1 tbsp. tomato paste
- ½ tsp ground cumin
- ¼ tsp ground ginger
- ¼ tsp ground cinnamon
- 1 tbsp. chili paste
- 4 cups low sodium vegetable stock
- 1 15-ounce can of coconut milk
- 10 ounces frozen cooked pumpkin
- Low fat yogurt to garnish
- Chili oil, to garnish

Directions:

1. Melt the coconut oil on medium heat in a large pot.
2. Add in the tomato paste, spices, and chili paste and fry for 1 minute.
3. Then pour in the stock and coconut milk and stir well to mix. Bring to a boil.
4. Add the pumpkin and cook for about 14 minutes until the pumpkin is fully heated through and soft.
5. Transfer soup to a blender, and blend on high until completely smooth.
6. Return to the pot, reheat, and then serve hot with a spoonful of yogurt and a drizzle of chili oil.

Nutrition Info:

- Info630 calories,35g carbs,17g protein,290mg sodium,54g fat.

Chicken Minestrone

Servings: 8
Cooking Time: 55 Mins
Ingredients:

- 20 ounces chicken and sage sausage, outer casing removed
- 1 tbsp. olive oil
- 2 tbsp. finely chopped garlic
- 1 tsp dried mixed Italian herbs
- 2 tbsp. fresh finely chopped oregano
- 2 shallots, diced
- 2 sweet carrots, peeled and diced
- 2 stalks celery, diced
- 5 cups low sodium chicken stock
- 1 14.5-ounce can chopped tomatoes
- 2 cups water
- ½ tsp dried chili flakes
- 1 bay leaf
- ½ cup baby marrow, diced
- 4 cups spinach, washed and destemmed
- 1 15-ounce can of cannellini beans, drained
- ¼ cup fresh basil, finely chopped, plus 8 sprigs to garnish
- ½ cup fresh parsley finely chopped

Directions:

1. Cut the sausage into pieces. Then heat the olive oil in a large deep pot and add in the sausage. Fry off for 6 minutes.
2. After 6 minutes, add in the garlic, herbs, shallots, carrot, and celery. Cook for about 5 minutes or until the shallots are translucent.
3. Pour in the stock, add the canned tomatoes, water, chili flakes, and bay leaf. Bring soup to a boil and cook on medium heat for 30 minutes.
4. Add the baby marrow, spinach, beans, and fresh chopped herbs. Stir in and cook for a further 15 minutes until the vegetables are all soft.
5. Scoop out the bay leaf and discard.
6. Serve hot spooned into bowls with a sprig of basil to garnish.

Nutrition Info:

- Info205 calories,19g carbs,16g protein,659mg sodium,8g fat.

Carrot Soup With Ginger

Servings:4
Cooking Time:x
Ingredients:

- 4 cups diced carrot
- 1 cup diced sweet potato
- 1 cup diced sweet onion
- 4 cups low-sodium vegetable or chicken broth
- 1 tablespoon minced fresh ginger
- 2 tablespoons chopped fresh parsley

Directions:

1. Combine carrot, sweet potato, onion, broth, and ginger in a small stockpot and bring to a boil over high heat. Once boiling, reduce heat to low and simmer, covered, for 30 minutes.
2. Remove from heat and purée using a blender or food processor. Serve immediately, garnished with parsley.

Nutrition Info:

- InfoCalories: 163,Fat: 2 g,Protein: 7 g,Sodium: 86 mg,Carbohydrates: 32 .

Chicken And Beet Soup

Servings:4
Cooking Time:25 Minutes
Ingredients:

- 1 tablespoon extra-virgin olive oil
- ¾ pound boneless, skinless chicken breasts, cut into 1-inch pieces
- 1 medium onion, diced
- 1 clove garlic, minced
- 2 cups low-sodium chicken broth
- 1 pound beets, peeled and grated
- 3 medium carrots, cut into ¼-inch-thick slices
- 1 teaspoon dried tarragon
- 1 teaspoon dried dill
- ¼ cup chopped fresh dill
- Freshly ground black pepper

Directions:

1. In a large nonstick Dutch oven or soup pot, heat the olive oil over medium-high until hot. Add the chicken, onion, and garlic and cook until the chicken is no longer pink, 5 to 7 minutes.
2. Add the broth, 2 cups water, the beets, carrots, tarragon, and dried dill and mix well. Bring to a boil, then reduce the heat, cover, and simmer until the vegetables are very tender, 15 to 20 minutes. Stir in the fresh dill and season to taste with black pepper.

Nutrition Info:

- InfoCalories 207,Sodium 303 mg,Total carbohydrates 20 g,Protein 21 .

Kale Soup With Lemon And Tuna

Servings:4
Cooking Time:x
Ingredients:

- 1 teaspoon olive oil
- 1 large shallot, minced
- 3 cloves garlic, minced
- Juice of 2 fresh lemons
- 8 cups chopped fresh kale
- 4 cups low-sodium chicken or vegetable broth
- 2 cans no-salt-added tuna, in water
- 1/4 cup wheat berries, uncooked
- 1 teaspoon salt-free herbes de Provence
- Freshly ground black pepper, to taste

Directions:

1. Heat oil in a stockpot over medium heat. Add the shallot and garlic and sauté for 2 minutes.
2. Add lemon juice and kale and cook, stirring, until kale has wilted, about 2 minutes.
3. Add the remaining ingredients and cover. Raise heat to high and bring to a boil. Once boiling, reduce heat to low and simmer for 20 minutes.
4. Remove from heat and serve immediately.

Nutrition Info:

- InfoCalories: 264,Fat: 5 g,Protein: 28 g,Sodium: 166 mg,Carbohydrates: 29 .

Apple Butternut Soup

Servings:6
Cooking Time:x
Ingredients:

- 6 cups diced butternut squash
- 2 cups diced apple
- 6 cups water
- 2 cups unsweetened apple juice
- 1/2 teaspoon ground cinnamon
- 1/8 teaspoon ground allspice

Directions:

1. Placed diced squash and apple into a stockpot, add the water and juice, and bring to a boil over high heat. Once boiling, reduce heat to medium-low, cover, and simmer for 20 minutes.
2. Remove from heat and purée using a blender or food processor.
3. Return soup to the pot, add spices, and stir to combine. Serve warm.

Nutrition Info:

- InfoCalories: 150,Fat: 0 g,Protein: 3 g,Sodium: 8 mg,Carbohydrates: 38 .

Quick And Easy Black Bean Soup

Servings:4
Cooking Time:15 Minutes
Ingredients:

- 2 cans black beans, rinsed and drained
- 1 tablespoon extra-virgin olive oil
- 1 medium onion, diced
- 4 cloves garlic, minced
- 2 cans no-salt-added (see Tip) fire-roasted tomatoes
- 1 cup low-sodium vegetable broth, plus more as needed
- 1 teaspoon ground cumin
- ½ teaspoon chili powder
- 1 tablespoon fresh lime juice
- Salt and freshly ground black pepper (optional)
- ½ cup chopped fresh cilantro

Directions:

1. In a food processor or blender, pulse half of the black beans until thickened but not fully pureed.
2. In a large pot or Dutch oven, heat the olive oil over medium-high heat. Add the onion and garlic and sauté until softened and lightly browned, 4 to 5 minutes.
3. Stir in the processed black beans, the remaining whole black beans, the tomatoes, broth, cumin, and chili powder. Bring to a simmer and cook for 10 to 15 minutes, until thickened. If the soup is too thick, add additional broth; if it is too thin, puree 1 to 2 cups of the soup in a blender and return it to the pot (or use an immersion blender to puree directly in the pot until your desired consistency is reached).
4. Remove from the heat and stir in the lime juice. Season with salt and pepper, if desired. Portion into 4 serving bowls and top with the cilantro.

Nutrition Info:

- InfoCalories 262,Sodium 59 mg,Total carbohydrates 44 g,Protein 13 .

Manhattan Snapper Chowder

Servings:10
Cooking Time:x
Ingredients:

- 1 tablespoon olive oil
- 1 medium yellow onion, chopped
- 2 medium carrots, cut into ½-inch dice
- 2 large celery ribs, cut into ½-inch dice
- 2 large red potatoes, scrubbed but unpeeled, cut into ½-inch dice
- 1 quart Homemade Chicken Broth (here) or canned low-sodium chicken broth
- 2 cups water
- ½ teaspoon freshly ground black pepper
- ½ teaspoon dried basil
- ¼ teaspoon dried thyme
- 1 bay leaf
- 2 cans no-salt-added diced tomatoes in juice, undrained
- 1 pound skinless snapper fillets, cut into bite-sized pieces
- Chopped fresh parsley, for serving (optional)

Directions:

1. Heat the oil in a large pot over medium heat. Add the onion, carrots, celery, and potatoes and cook, stirring often, until the onions are tender, about 5 minutes. Stir in the broth, water, pepper, basil, thyme, and bay leaf. Bring to a boil over high heat. Reduce the heat and simmer until the potatoes are almost tender, about 15 minutes. Stir in the tomatoes with their juice and simmer until the potatoes are tender, about 10 minutes more.
2. Add the snapper and cook until opaque, about 3 minutes. Discard the bay leaf. Ladle into bowls, sprinkle with parsley (if using), and serve hot.

Nutrition Info:

- Info143 calories,14 g protein,17 g carbohydrates,2 g fat,714 mg sodiu.

Chicken, Corn, And Black Bean Chili

Servings:8
Cooking Time:x
Ingredients:

- 2 cans no-salt-added black beans
- 2 teaspoons olive oil
- 1 pound boneless, skinless chicken breasts, cut into 1⁄2-inch cubes
- 1 medium red onion, diced
- 3 cloves garlic, minced
- 1 medium green bell pepper, diced
- 1 medium red bell pepper, diced
- 1 can salt-free tomato paste
- 2 tablespoons salt-free chili powder
- 1 teaspoon ground cumin
- 2 cups low-sodium chicken broth
- 2 cups frozen corn kernels
- 1⁄4 cup chopped fresh cilantro
- Freshly ground black pepper, to taste

Directions:

1. Drain and rinse beans and set aside.
2. Heat oil in a large sauté pan over medium heat. Add chicken and sauté until the outside is no longer pink, approximately 3–5 minutes.
3. Add the onion and garlic and sauté for 2 minutes. Add the bell peppers and sauté for 2 minutes.
4. Stir in the tomato paste, chili powder, cumin, broth, and black beans. Raise heat to high and bring to a boil.
5. Once boiling, reduce heat to medium-low, cover, and simmer for 20 minutes.
6. Stir in the corn kernels, cover, and continue cooking for 5 minutes.
7. Remove from heat, stir in the cilantro, and season to taste with freshly ground black pepper. Serve immediately.

Nutrition Info:

- InfoCalories: 309,Fat: 4 g,Protein: 28 g,Sodium: 81 mg,Carbohydrates: 42 .

Banana Coconut Soup With Tropical Fruit

Servings:4
Cooking Time:x
Ingredients:

- 2 medium ripe bananas
- 1 can light coconut milk
- 1 tablespoon honey
- 1⁄8 teaspoon ground cardamom
- 1 ripe mango, diced
- 1 ripe kiwi, sliced
- 2 cups cubed fresh pineapple

Directions:

1. Peel the bananas, place in a food processor, and purée.
2. Add the coconut milk and pulse to combine.
3. Pour contents of food processor into a small mixing bowl. Add the honey and cardamom and stir to combine.
4. Divide evenly between 4 bowls, then top with fresh fruit. Serve immediately.

Nutrition Info:

- InfoCalories: 235,Fat: 7 g,Protein: 1 g,Sodium: 24 mg,Carbohydrates: 42 .

Desserts

Banana Chocolate Dessert Smoothie

Servings: 2
Cooking Time:x
Ingredients:

- 1 medium frozen banana, chopped
- 3/4 cup unsweetened almond milk
- 1/4 cup water
- 1 1/2 tablespoons unsweetened cocoa powder
- 1/8 teaspoon ground cinnamon
- 1 tablespoon raw, unsalted almond butter
- 3 drops almond extract
- 3–4 ice cubes
- Sprig of fresh mint

Directions:

1. Place all ingredients except the mint in a blender, and blend on high for about a minute. For a thicker, slushier smoothie, add more ice. Garnish with fresh mint.

Nutrition Info:

- InfoCalories 139,Total Fat 7 g,Sodium 71 mg,Total Carbohydrate 21 g,Protein 3 .

Vegan Rice Pudding

Servings:8
Cooking Time:x
Ingredients:

- 1 quart vanilla nondairy milk
- 1 cup basmati or jasmine rice, rinsed
- 1/4 cup sugar
- 1 teaspoon pure vanilla extract
- 1/8 teaspoon pure almond extract
- 1/2 teaspoon ground cinnamon
- 1/8 teaspoon ground cardamom

Directions:

1. Measure all of the ingredients into a saucepan and stir well to combine. Bring to a boil over medium-high heat.
2. Once boiling, reduce heat to low and simmer, stirring very frequently, about 15–20 minutes.
3. Remove from heat and cool. Serve sprinkled with ground cinnamon if desired.

Nutrition Info:

- InfoCalories: 148,Fat: 2 g,Protein: 4 g,Sodium: 48 mg,Carbohydrates: 26 .

Berry Buttermilk Panna Cotta

Servings: 6
Cooking Time: 7 Mins
Ingredients:

- 2 ¾ cups buttermilk
- 3 tsp plain gelatin powder
- ¼ cup plus 2 tbsp. almond milk
- ½ cup maple syrup
- ½ tsp vanilla essence
- Flavorless oil in a spray bottle
- ½ cup fresh blueberries
- ½ cup fresh strawberries, cut into quarters

Directions:

1. Gently warm the buttermilk in a small pot over very low heat. Do NOT boil or overheat, as it will curdle.
2. Then sponge the gelatin by dissolving the gelatin powder in the almond milk in a small glass bowl. Let it sit and absorb for 5 minutes. Place the glass bowl over a pot of very gently simmering water and stir until the gelatin mixture melts completely.
3. Slowly pour the gelatin mixture into the warmed buttermilk and whisk to combine. Then add the maple syrup and vanilla essence and whisk again. Transfer the mixture into a jug and set aside.
4. Lightly oil 6 ramekins and then pour the buttermilk mixture equally into all 6. Place the ramekins on a small tray and cover.
5. Allow the Panna Cottas to set in the fridge for at least 4 hours, but up to 2 days.
6. When ready to serve, very gently loosen the sides of the Panna Cottas with a sharp knife. Run the knife to the bottom to release any air pockets.
7. Turn the ramekins slowly upside-down over the serving plate to gently release the finished product.
8. Garnish equally with the fresh berries and enjoy chilled.

Nutrition Info:

- Info148 calories,30g carbs,5g protein,127mg sodium,1g fat.

Zucchini Muffins

Servings: 12
Cooking Time:x
Ingredients:

- 2/3 cup extra virgin olive oil
- 2 large eggs
- 1/2 cup firmly packed brown sugar
- 1/4 cup honey
- 1 teaspoon vanilla extract
- 1 cup all-purpose flour
- 1 cup whole wheat flour
- 1/2 teaspoon baking soda
- 1/2 teaspoon baking powder
- 1/8 teaspoon sea salt
- 2 teaspoons ground cinnamon
- 2 1/2 cups shredded zucchini
- 1/4 cup old-fashioned oats
- 1/2 cup toasted chopped walnuts
- 1/4 cup flaxseeds

Directions:

1. Preheat the oven to 375°F. Spray the muffin tin with olive oil spray.
2. In a large bowl, whisk the oil with the eggs, sugar, honey, and vanilla until slightly creamy. In a separate large bowl, sift the flours, baking soda, baking powder, salt, and cinnamon. Add the sifted ingredients to the wet ingredients, stirring with a spatula until blended. Fold in the shredded zucchini, oats, walnuts, and flaxseeds. Stir with a spatula until there are no more dry spots in the batter. Scoop into the muffin cups, sprinkle with cinnamon, and bake for 20 to 22 minutes, or until a toothpick inserted comes out clean.

Nutrition Info:

- InfoCalories 362,Total Fat 25 g,Sodium 91 mg,Total Carbohydrate 39 g,Protein 5 .

Mini Banana Vegan Muffins

Servings: 6
Cooking Time:x
Ingredients:

- 1/2 cup whole wheat flour
- 1/4 cup all-purpose flour
- 1/2 teaspoon baking soda
- /2 teaspoon baking powder
- 1/2 teaspoon ground cinnamon
- 1/8 teaspoon salt
- 2 medium ripe bananas
- 1/4 cup firmly packed brown sugar
- 1/8 cup unsweetened applesauce
- 1/8 teaspoon vanilla extract
- 1 1/2 tablespoons extra virgin olive oil
- 1/4 cup toasted chopped walnuts

Directions:

1. Preheat the oven to 375°F. Spray a mini muffin pan with olive oil spray.
2. In a large bowl, sift together the flours, baking soda, baking powder, cinnamon, and salt. In a separate large bowl, mash the bananas, and add the brown sugar, applesauce, vanilla, and oil. Stir the flour mixture into the banana mixture just until moistened. Do not overstir the batter. Fold in the walnuts.
3. Using a teaspoon, spoon the batter into the prepared muffin cups. Bake for 15 to 18 minutes, or until a toothpick inserted into center of a muffin comes out clean. Do not overbake.

Nutrition Info:

- InfoCalories 188,Total Fat 7 g,Sodium 150 mg,Total Carbohydrate 34 g,Protein 3 .

Delicious Oatmeal Cookies

Servings:36
Cooking Time:x
Ingredients:

- 1/2 cup unsalted butter, at room temperature
- 3/4 cup firmly packed brown sugar
- 2 large eggs
- 1 teaspoon vanilla extract
- 1 cup whole wheat flour
- 1/2 cup brown rice flour
- 3 tablespoons flaxseeds
- 1 teaspoon baking soda
- 1/2 teaspoon ground cinnamon
- 1/8 teaspoon ground ginger
- 1/8 teaspoon ground nutmeg
- 3 cups old-fashioned oats
- 1 cup raisins
- 1 cup toasted chopped walnuts

Directions:

1. Preheat the oven to 350°F.
2. In a large bowl, beat the butter and sugar with an electric mixer on medium speed until creamy. Add the eggs and vanilla, and beat well. In a separate large bowl, combine the flours, flaxseeds, baking soda, cinnamon, ginger, and nutmeg. Add the dry mixture in three batches to the wet mixture, incorporating evenly after each batch. Add the oats, raisins, and walnuts, and mix by hand with a spatula until evenly incorporated.
3. Drop the dough by rounded tablespoonful onto ungreased cookie sheets. Be careful not to overcrowd them.
4. Bake 8 to 10 minutes, or until light golden brown. Cool 1 minute on the cookie sheets, and then transfer to a wire rack. Repeat process for the second batch of cookies. Cool completely, and store tightly covered.

Nutrition Info:

- InfoCalories 130,Total Fat 6 g,Sodium 43 mg,Total Carbohydrate 23 g,Protein 3 .

Healthy Mini Cheesecakes With Vanilla Wafer Almond Crust

Servings: 6
Cooking Time:x

Ingredients:

- CRUST
- 3 1/2 ounces vanilla wafers
- 1/2 cup toasted, slivered almonds
- 1/2 teaspoon ground cinnamon
- 1/4 cup flaxseeds
- 4 tablespoons extra virgin olive oil
- CHEESECAKE BATTER
- 1 cup whole milk ricotta cheese
- 2 cups low-fat plain Greek yogurt
- 1 tablespoon maple syrup
- Grated zest of 1/2 lime
- Grated zest of 1/2 lemon
- Juice of 1/2 lemon
- 1 teaspoon vanilla extract
- 1 egg, beaten
- 1/4 cup flour

Directions:

1. Preheat the oven to 350°F.
2. To make the crust, mix the wafers, almonds, cinnamon, and flaxseeds in a food processor until the mixture looks like flour. Drizzle in oil until the mixture holds together. Grease a 12-cup muffin tin with olive oil spray. Divide the mixture among the cups, and mold the crust inside each with your fingers, making the crust go all the way up the sides. Bake 8 to 10 minutes, or until the crusts darken and you can smell them. Remove from the oven, and let cool completely.
3. To make the batter, in a large bowl whisk together all the ingredients except the egg and flour until there are no lumps. Add the beaten egg to the batter, and mix thoroughly. Add the flour, mixing with a spatula until incorporated.
4. Pour the batter into the cooled crusts, return to the 350°F oven, and bake for an additional 15 to 20 minutes, or until you shake the pan and the filling doesn't jiggle. Remove from the oven, and cool completely.
5. Serving suggestion: If crumbs get stuck to the bottom of the pan when you're removing the mini cheesecakes, use the crumbs to top the cheesecakes. Other toppings include fresh blueberries, blackberries, and raspberries.

Nutrition Info:

- InfoCalories 367,Total Fat 23 g,Sodium 134 mg,Total Carbohydrate 25 g,Protein 16 .

Chewy Pumpkin Oatmeal Raisin Cookies

Servings:4
Cooking Time: 16 Minutes

Ingredients:

- 1 cup pumpkin purée
- 1 2/3 cups sugar
- 2 tablespoons molasses
- 1 1/2 teaspoons pure vanilla extract
- 2/3 cup canola oil
- 1 tablespoon ground flaxseed
- 2 teaspoons Ener-G Baking Soda Substitute
- 1 teaspoon ground cinnamon
- 1/2 teaspoon ground nutmeg
- 1 cup unbleached all-purpose flour
- 1 cup white whole-wheat flour
- 1 1/3 cups rolled or quick oats
- 1 cup seedless raisins

Directions:

1. Preheat oven to 350°F. Spray 2 baking sheets lightly with oil and set aside.
2. Measure the ingredients into a large mixing bowl and stir together using a rubber spatula, scraping the bottom and sides of the bowl to incorporate everything fully.
3. Scoop batter out by tablespoons—a small retractable ice cream scoop works wonderfully here—and place on the prepared baking sheets.
4. Place sheets on middle rack in oven and bake 16 minutes. Remove from oven and transfer cookies to a wire rack to cool.
5. Repeat process with remaining batter. Once cool, store cookies in an airtight container.

Nutrition Info:

- InfoCalories: 97,Fat: 3 g,Protein: 1 g,Sodium: 1 millig,Carbohydrates: 16 .

Tracie's Whoopie Pies

Servings:9
Cooking Time:x
Ingredients:

- 1 1⁄2 cups unbleached all-purpose flour
- 1⁄2 cup white whole-wheat flour
- 3⁄4 cup sugar
- 1⁄3 cup unsweetened cocoa powder
- 2 teaspoons sodium-free baking soda
- 1 egg white
- 1⁄3 cup canola oil
- 3⁄4 cup low-fat milk
- 4 tablespoons unsalted butter
- 2 teaspoons pure vanilla extract
- 6 tablespoons marshmallow fluff
- 2 cups powdered sugar

Directions:

1. Preheat oven to 375°F. Line a large baking sheet with parchment and set aside.
2. Place the flours, sugar, cocoa powder, and baking soda into a mixing bowl and whisk to combine.
3. Add the egg white, oil, and milk and beat well.
4. Drop by heaping tablespoonfuls onto the prepared baking sheet. Place sheet on middle rack in oven and bake for 10 minutes.
5. Remove sheet from oven. Remove cookie halves from baking sheet and transfer to a wire rack to cool. Repeat process with remaining batter.
6. Melt the butter in a saucepan over medium heat. Once melted, remove from heat, add the remaining ingredients, and stir well to combine. If frosting is too dry, add a tiny bit of low-fat milk and beat until smooth.
7. Once the cookie halves have cooled, make sandwiches out of them by spreading filling on one half and sandwiching with another. Store in an airtight container or wrap in plastic.

Nutrition Info:

- InfoCalories: 408,Fat: 14 g,Protein: 4 g,Sodium: 19 mg,Carbohydrates: 68 .

Fruit Kebabs

Servings:8
Cooking Time:x
Ingredients:

- 3 tablespoons lime juice
- 3 tablespoons orange juice
- 1 tablespoon jarred minced ginger
- ¾ cup cantaloupe chunks
- ¾ cup star fruit, cut into ½-inch slices
- ¾ cup strawberries
- ¾ cup peach chunks
- One 6-ounce container nonfat vanilla yogurt
- ⅛ teaspoon cayenne pepper

Directions:

1. In a shallow lasagna pan, combine lime juice, orange juice, and ginger.
2. Thread cantaloupe, star fruit, strawberries, and peaches onto eight skewers. Arrange on top of juice mixture and turn to coat.
3. In a small bowl, combine yogurt and cayenne.
4. Remove skewers from marinade, and serve with spiced yogurt.

Nutrition Info:

- InfoCalories: 91,Fat: 1 GRAM,Sodium: 20 ml,Carbs: 21 g,Protein: 2 .

Cucumber-watermelon Cooler

Servings: 4
Cooking Time:x
Ingredients:

* 5 cups chopped seedless watermelon
* 1 cup chopped unpeeled cucumber
* 10 fresh mint leaves
* Juice of 1/2 lime

Directions:

1. Blend the watermelon and cucumber in the blender, in batches if necessary. Add the mint and lime juice in the last blend. Serve chilled as a beverage or summer soup, or freeze in Popsicle molds for a light treat.

Nutrition Info:

* InfoCalories 66,Total Fat 0.9 g,Sodium 5 mg,Total Carbohydrate 15 g,Protein 2 .

Pumpkin Seed Brittle

Servings:10
Cooking Time: 25 Minutes
Ingredients:

* ½ teaspoon cayenne pepper
* ¼ teaspoon grated nutmeg
* 1 cup roasted, unsalted pumpkin seeds
* 1 cup granulated stevia
* ½ cup granulated sugar
* ¼ cup water

Directions:

1. Line a jelly roll pan with parchment paper or a baking mat. Combine cayenne, nutmeg, and pumpkin seeds in a small bowl and set aside.
2. In a large sauté pan, combine the stevia, sugar, and water, and cook over high heat, stirring constantly with a silicone spatula, until the mixture begins to boil, about 6 minutes. Using a pastry brush, swab down sides of pan so all sugar cooks evenly. Cook 3 more minutes without stirring.
3. Reduce heat to medium. Cook for another 15 to 20 minutes, checking frequently, until the mixture turns a golden, light brown color. Remove from heat.
4. Using a silicone spatula, quickly stir the pumpkin seed mixture into the sugar mixture. Pour into the prepared baking pan, and press firmly with the spatula to make a single, even layer.
5. Cool completely, then break into pieces and serve.

Nutrition Info:

* InfoCalories: 20,Fat: 0 g,Sodium: 7 ml,Carbs: 4 g,Protein: 0 .

Berry Sundae

Servings: 6
Cooking Time:x
Ingredients:

* 1 1/2 cups coarsely chopped strawberries
* 1 1/2 cups blueberries
* 1 1/2 cups raspberries
* 1 1/2 tablespoons balsamic vinegar
* Pinch of cracked black pepper
* 1 1/2 teaspoons grated lemon zest
* 1 1/2 teaspoons grated orange zest
* Juice of 1/2 orange
* 1/2 teaspoon vanilla extract
* 3 cups low-fat plain Greek yogurt
* 6 tablespoons sliced toasted almonds

Directions:

1. Place all ingredients except the yogurt and almonds in a large pot over medium heat, and cook until the liquid begins to bubble. Decrease the heat to low, and boil the mixture for about 15 minutes, or until it thickens. The berries will naturally fall apart, leaving a slightly chunky sauce. For a smoother sauce, crush the berries with a fork or masher. Remove from the heat. Place 1/2 cup of yogurt into six bowls, and top with sauce and toasted almonds.

Nutrition Info:

* InfoCalories 163,Total Fat 4 g,Sodium 47 mg,Total Carbohydrate 20 g,Protein 14 .

Mexican Fruit Salad

Servings: 4
Cooking Time:x
Ingredients:

- 1/2 cantaloupe, cut into bite-sized cubes
- 5 large strawberries, sliced
- 2 kiwifruit, peeled, halved, and sliced
- 1 large banana, sliced
- 1/2 cup halved green and red grapes
- 1 cup low-fat cottage cheese
- 1/4 cup raisins
- 3 tablespoons honey
- 1/2 cup low-sugar granola

Directions:
1. Place all cut fruit in a large bowl. Top with cottage cheese and raisins, and then drizzle honey over the top. Let sit for 30 minutes in the refrigerator, and then toss before spooning into serving bowls. Top each serving with granola.

Nutrition Info:
- InfoCalories 295,Total Fat 5 g,Sodium 251 mg,Total Carbohydrate 56 g,Protein 11 .

Sweet Potato Dessert

Servings: 1
Cooking Time:x
Ingredients:

- 1 small or 1/2 large sweet potato
- 1/2 cup low-fat vanilla yogurt
- 1/4 teaspoon ground cinnamon
- 2 tablespoons sliced almonds

Directions:
1. Preheat the oven to 400°F. Pierce the sweet potato with a fork in several places, wrap in foil, and place on a cookie sheet to catch any juicy drippings. Bake for about 30 to 40 minutes, or until the sweet potato is soft and squishy to the touch. Remove from the oven, unwrap, and place in a bowl. Cut open down the middle, and top with the yogurt, cinnamon, and almonds.

Nutrition Info:
- InfoCalories 179,Total Fat 6 g,Sodium 108 mg,Total Carbohydrate 23 g,Protein 9 .

Vegan Date Nut Loaf

Servings: 10
Cooking Time:x
Ingredients:

- 1 cup chopped pitted dates
- 1 cup coarsely chopped unsalted pecans
- 1 1/2 teaspoons baking soda
- 1/8 teaspoon salt
- 3 tablespoons extra virgin olive oil
- 3/4 cup boiling water
- 1 /2 medium ripe bananas, mashed
- 1/4 cup firmly packed brown sugar
- 1 teaspoon vanilla extract
- 1/2 teaspoon ground cinnamon
- 1/8 teaspoon ground nutmeg
- 1/8 teaspoon ground ginger
- 1 1/2 cups whole wheat flour

Directions:
1. Preheat the oven to 350°F. Spray an 8- by 4-inch loaf pan with olive oil spray.
2. In a large bowl, combine the dates, pecans, baking soda, salt, and oil. Pour the boiling water over the mixture, and stir to incorporate. Let stand for 15 minutes.
3. In a separate large bowl, mash the bananas with a fork, and add the sugar, vanilla, cinnamon, nutmeg, and ginger. Stir with a spoon. Add the flour, and stir. Add the date mixture, folding in the ingredients with a spatula until the batter is well blended. Be careful not to overstir once all ingredients are incorporated. Spoon the mixture into the loaf pan, and bake for 35 to 45 minutes, or until an inserted toothpick comes out clean. Check the loaf after 35 minutes. The bread will continue to bake after it is removed from the oven, so be careful not to overbake. Once the loaf has cooled slightly, slide a knife around the edges of the pan, and turn the loaf onto a rack to cool completely. Cut into 10 slices.

Nutrition Info:
- InfoCalories 268,Total Fat 13 g,Sodium 22 mg,Total Carbohydrate 40 g,Protein 4 .

Blueberry Pudding Cake

Servings:6
Cooking Time:x
Ingredients:

- 3 cups fresh ripe blueberries
- ¾ cup sugar, divided
- 1 tablespoon freshly squeezed lemon juice
- 6 tablespoons unsalted butter, softened
- 2 teaspoons pure vanilla extract
- 1 teaspoon freshly grated lemon zest
- 1 egg white
- 1½ teaspoons sodium-free baking powder
- 2 tablespoons low-fat milk
- ⅔ cup unbleached all-purpose flour

Directions:

1. Preheat oven to 375°F. Spray an 8-inch square baking pan lightly with oil and set aside.
2. Place blueberries into a mixing bowl. Add ¼ cup sugar and lemon juice and toss well to coat.
3. Pour berries into the baking dish, place on middle rack in oven, and bake for 10 minutes. Remove from oven and set aside.
4. Place the butter and remaining ½ cup sugar into a mixing bowl and beat to combine.
5. Add the vanilla, lemon zest, and egg white and mix well.
6. Add the baking powder and milk and stir. Gradually add in the flour, mixing until combined.
7. Pour batter over the cooked blueberries. Place pan on middle rack in oven and bake for 20 minutes, until golden brown.
8. Remove from oven and place pan on wire rack to cool. Serve warm or cool.

Nutrition Info:

- InfoCalories: 300,Fat: 12 g,Protein: 2 g,Sodium: 14 mg,Carbohydrates: 46 .

Fruited Oatmeal Cookies

Servings:40
Cooking Time: 12 Minutes
Ingredients:

- 1⅓ cups uncooked old-fashioned oats or quick-cooking rolled oats
- 1 cup whole-wheat flour
- 1 teaspoon baking powder
- 1 teaspoon ground cinnamon
- ¼ teaspoon ground mace
- ½ cup loosely packed brown sugar
- ⅓ cup plain low-fat yogurt
- 2 tablespoons canola oil
- 1 egg
- 1 teaspoon vanilla extract
- ½ cup mixed dried fruit
- ½ cup dark chocolate chips

Directions:

1. Preheat oven to 350°F. Line two baking sheets with baking mats or parchment paper.
2. In a medium bowl, stir together oats, flour, baking powder, cinnamon, mace, and sugar.
3. In a large bowl, stir together yogurt, oil, egg, and vanilla. Add flour mixture to yogurt mixture. Using a spatula, mix until just combined. Stir in dried fruit and chocolate chips.
4. Using a tablespoon, drop cookie dough onto baking sheet about 2 inches apart.
5. Bake 10 to 12 minutes, until lightly browned. Remove from oven and cool on a wire rack.

Nutrition Info:

- InfoCalories: 78,Fat: 3 g,Sodium: 4 ml,Carbs: 12 g,Protein: 2 .

Grilled Apricots With Cinnamon

Servings: 4
Cooking Time:x
Ingredients:

- 4 large apricots, halved and pitted
- 1 tablespoon extra virgin olive oil
- 1/4 teaspoon ground cinnamon

Directions:

1. Brush both sides of each apricot half with oil, and place flat side down on a heated grill or grill pan. Grill for about 4 minutes, turn the apricot halves over, and cook for a few more minutes, until soft. Remove the apricots from the grill, and sprinkle with cinnamon. Enjoy warm or chilled.

Nutrition Info:

- InfoCalories 47,Total Fat 4 g,Sodium 0.4 mg,Total Carbohydrate 4 g,Protein 0.5 .

Choco-fudge Cookies

Servings: 12
Cooking Time: 15 Mins
Ingredients:

- 15 ounces cooked chickpeas, rinsed and drained
- 3 tbsp. smooth pecan nut butter
- ½ cup cocoa powder, unsweetened
- ½ cup rolled oats
- ¼ cup pumpkin puree
- 1 tsp vanilla essence
- 1 tsp cinnamon
- 1 tsp baking powder
- ¼ cup stevia
- 2 tbsp. almond milk
- 6 tbsp. egg whites
- ½ tsp honey
- Canola oil in a spray bottle

Directions:

1. Preheat the oven to 350ºF
2. Using a high-powered blender, blend all the ingredients to form a firm cookie dough.
3. Lightly grease a baking sheet, then spoon out 12 cookies into the sheet. Press them down slightly and then bake for about 15 minutes, or until firm.
4. Let cool and serve.

Nutrition Info:

- Info65 calories,12g carbs,5g protein,78mg sodium,1g fat.

6-WEEK Meal Plan

Day 1
Breakfast: Pumpkin Pancakes
Lunch: Parmesan Crusted Pork
Dinner: Mexican Chicken Breast With Tomatillo Salsa

Day 2
Breakfast: Scrambled Eggs With Apples, Sage, And Swiss Cheese
Lunch: Pressure Cooker Beef Bourguignon
Dinner: Chicken, Black Bean, And Veggie Soft Tacos

Day 3
Breakfast: Brown Sugar Cinnamon Oatmeal
Lunch: Pork Chops With Sweet-and-sour Cabbage
Dinner: Cod With Grapefruit, Avocado, And Fennel Salad

Day 4
Breakfast: Cream Of Buckwheat Breakfast Cereal With Fruit And Flaxseed
Lunch: Dirty Rice
Dinner: Coconut Cauliflower Curry

Day 5
Breakfast: Swiss Cheese And Chive Mini Quiches
Lunch: Spiced Roast Eye Of Round
Dinner:30-minute Vegetarian Pizza

Day 6
Breakfast: Oven-baked Apple Pancake
Lunch: Beef-and-bean Chili
Dinner: Coconut Collards With Sweet Potatoes And Black Beans

Day 7
Breakfast: Avo Trout Toastie
Lunch: Chinese-style Beef Stir-fry
Dinner: Summer Vegetable Risotto

Day 8
Breakfast: Apples And Cinnamon Oatmeal
Lunch: Beef With Bok Choy
Dinner: Chili Stuffed Baked Potatoes

Day 9
Breakfast:2-minute Egg And Vegetable Breakfast Mug
Lunch: Whole-grain Rotini With Pork, Pumpkin, And Sage
Dinner: Chilled Cucumber-and-avocado Soup With Dill

Day 10
Breakfast: Broccoli Omelet
Lunch: Basil Pesto
Dinner: Spinach Burgers

Day 11
Breakfast: Quinoa And Spinach Power Salad
Lunch: Spicy Sichuan Orange Beef Vegetable Stir-fry
Dinner: Coconut Rice And White Beans

Day 12
Breakfast: Strawberry Yogurt Smoothie
Lunch: Sweet And Savory Apple-cinnamon Baked Pork Chops
Dinner: Amazing Veggie Casserole

Day 13
Breakfast: Green Apple Pie Protein Smoothie
Lunch: Sweet & Sour Pork Chops
Dinner: Crustless Vegan Mushroom And Sweet Potato Mini Quiches

Day 14
Breakfast: Chocolate-cherry Smoothie Bowl
Lunch: Beef And Mushrooms With Sour Cream–dill Sauce
Dinner: Speedy Samosa Pasta

Day 15

Breakfast: Summer Veg Brekkie Cup
Lunch: Pork Medallions With Spring Succotash
Dinner: Butternut-squash Macaroni And Cheese

Day 16

Breakfast: Kale And Apple Smoothie
Lunch: Apple-cinnamon Baked Pork Chops
Dinner: Black Bean Mushroom Burgers

Day 17

Breakfast: Ricotta Breakfast Toast Two Ways
Lunch: Orange-beef Stir-fry
Dinner: Linguine With Plum Tomatoes, Mushrooms, And Tempeh

Day 18

Breakfast: Broccoli And Pepper Jack Omelet
Lunch: Turkey Mini Meat Loaf With Dijon Glaze
Dinner: Quinoa With Mixed Vegetables And Cilantro Peanut Pesto

Day 19

Breakfast: Raspberry Polenta Waffles
Lunch: Turkey Cutlets With Lemon And Basil Sauce
Dinner: North-african Garbanzo Bean Tagine

Day 20

Breakfast: Pumpkin Waffles
Lunch: Moo Shu Chicken And Vegetable Wraps
Dinner: Pasta With Tomatoes And Peas

Day 21

Breakfast: Grilled Rustic Corn
Lunch: Chicken And Apple Curry
Dinner: Black-eyed Peas And Greens Power Salad

Day 22

Breakfast: Apple Walnut Wheat Stuffing
Lunch: Turkey And Brown Rice Stuffed Peppers
Dinner: Lentil And Goat Cheese Salad

Day 23

Breakfast: Cauliflower Mashed "potatoes"
Lunch: Turkey-spinach Meatballs With Tomato Sauce
Dinner: Warm Potato Salad With Spinach

Day 24

Breakfast: Whole-grain Crackers
Lunch: Spicy Chicken Mac N Cheese
Dinner: Salad Niçoise

Day 25

Breakfast: Southwestern Bean-and-pepper Salad
Lunch: Low-sodium Kung Pao Chicken
Dinner: Chinese Chicken Salad

Day 26

Breakfast: Tart Apple Salad With Fennel And Honey Yogurt Dressing
Lunch: Nut-crusted Chicken
Dinner: Tarragon Chicken Salad With Grapes And Almonds

Day 27

Breakfast: Italian Kale And White Beans
Lunch: Ground Turkey Sloppy Joes
Dinner: Roasted Beet Salad With Yogurt-dill Dressing

Day 28

Breakfast: Guacamole With No-salt Corn Chips
Lunch: Crispy Turkey In Tomato Sauce
Dinner: Bean Salad With Orange Vinaigrette

Day 29

Breakfast: Broccoli Ziti
Lunch: Turkey And Brown Rice–stuffed Peppers
Dinner: Tomato Cucumber Basil Salad

Day 30

Breakfast: Homemade Soft Pretzels
Lunch: Cheesy Turkey Filled Pasta Shells
Dinner: Tuna And White Bean Salad

Day 31

Breakfast: Maple Mocha Frappe
Lunch: Sloppy Toms
Dinner: Iceberg Lettuce Wedge With Russian Dressing

Day 32

Breakfast: Simple Autumn Salad
Lunch: Classic Poached Chicken
Dinner: Chipotle Chicken Chili Taco Salad

Day 33

Breakfast: Vegan Caesar Salad Dressing
Lunch: Japanese Yellowfin Tuna
Dinner: Creamy Low-sodium Coleslaw

Day 34

Breakfast: Apple Honey Mustard Vinaigrette
Lunch: Roasted Salmon Fillets With Basil Drizzle
Dinner: Roast Beef Salad With Beets, Apple, And Horseradish

Day 35

Breakfast: Stir-fried Cabbage And Noodles
Lunch: Tuna With Fennel And Potatoes
Dinner: American-style French Dressing

Day 36

Breakfast: Black Bean And Apple Salsa
Lunch: Sea Scallops And Vegetables With Ginger Sauce
Dinner: Warm Asian Slaw

Day 37

Breakfast: Mini Shepherd's Pies
Lunch: Halibut With Spring Vegetables
Dinner: Shrimp, Mango, And Black Bean Salad

Day 38

Breakfast: Asian-inspired Mini Meatloaves With Salt-free Hoisin Glaze
Lunch: Haddock Tacos With Mexican Slaw
Dinner: Kale, Pear, And Bulgur Salad

Day 39

Breakfast: Beef And Bulgur Meat Loaf
Lunch: Brown Rice Paella With Cod, Shrimp, And Asparagus
Dinner: Asian Shrimp Salad

Day 40

Breakfast: Seasoned Turkey Burgers With Sautéed Mushrooms And Swiss
Lunch: Shrimp With Corn Hash
Dinner: Weeknight Tossed Green Salad

Day 41

Breakfast: Sweet Chili Chicken Wrap
Lunch: Fish Tacos With Lime-cilantro Slaw
Dinner: Tomato Garlic Dressing

Day 42

Breakfast: Louisiana Turkey Burgers
Lunch: Cajun Crusted Trout
Dinner: Barley Soup With Asparagus And Mushrooms

INDEX

Cheesy Shrimp Pasta 55
Cheesy Turkey Filled Pasta Shells 45
Chewy Pumpkin Oatmeal Raisin Cookies 89
Chicken And Apple Curry 38
Chicken And Beet Soup 82
Chicken Minestrone 81
Chicken, Black Bean, And Veggie Soft Tacos 46
Chicken, Corn, And Black Bean Chili 85
Chili Stuffed Baked Potatoes 59
Chilled Cucumber-and-avocado Soup With Dill 60
Chinese Chicken Salad 68
Chinese-style Beef Stir-fry 30
Chipotle Chicken Chili Taco Salad 72
Choco-fudge Cookies 94
Chocolate-cherry Smoothie Bowl 16
Classic Poached Chicken 46
Coconut Cauliflower Curry 57
Coconut Collards With Sweet Potatoes And Black Beans 58
Coconut Rice And White Beans 61
Cod With Grapefruit, Avocado, And Fennel Salad 48
Cream Of Buckwheat Breakfast Cereal With Fruit And Flaxseed 12
Creamy Low-sodium Coleslaw 72
Crispy Turkey In Tomato Sauce 44
Crunchy Coated Nuts 26
Crustless Vegan Mushroom And Sweet Potato Mini Quiches 62
Cucumber-watermelon Cooler 91

D

Delicious Oatmeal Cookies 88
Dirty Rice 28

F

Fish Tacos With Lime-cilantro Slaw 52
Freshwater Fish Casserole 54
Fruit Kebabs 90
Fruited Oatmeal Cookies 93

G

Garden Tomato Soup 79
Green Apple Pie Protein Smoothie 15
Grilled Apricots With Cinnamon 94
Grilled Rustic Corn 19
Ground Turkey Sloppy Joes 43
Guacamole With No-salt Corn Chips 22

H

Haddock Tacos With Mexican Slaw 50
Halibut With Spring Vegetables 50
Healthy Fish And Chips 55

Healthy Mini Cheesecakes With Vanilla Wafer Almond Crust 89
Hearty Vegetable Beef Soup 77
Homemade Clam Chowder 80
Homemade Soft Pretzels 23

I

Iceberg Lettuce Wedge With Russian Dressing 71
Italian Kale And White Beans 22

J

Japanese Yellowfin Tuna 47

K

Kale And Apple Smoothie 17
Kale Soup With Lemon And Tuna 83
Kale, Pear, And Bulgur Salad 74

L

Lentil And Goat Cheese Salad 67
Linguine With Plum Tomatoes, Mushrooms, And Tempeh 64
Louisiana Turkey Burgers 43
Low-sodium Kung Pao Chicken 41

M

Manhattan Snapper Chowder 84
Maple Mocha Frappe 24
Marinara Sauce 58
Mexican Chicken Breast With Tomatillo Salsa 42
Mexican Fruit Salad 92
Mini Banana Vegan Muffins 88
Mini Shepherd's Pies 31
Moo Shu Chicken And Vegetable Wraps 38

N

New England Clam Chowder 79
New York Chowder 76
North-african Garbanzo Bean Tagine 65
Nut-crusted Chicken 42

O

Orange-beef Stir-fry 36
Oven-baked Apple Pancake 13

P

Parmesan Crusted Pork 27
Pasta With Tomatoes And Peas 66
Pork Chops With Sweet-and-sour Cabbage 28
Pork Medallions With Spring Succotash 35
Pressure Cooker Beef Bourguignon 27
Pumpkin And Coconut Soup 81
Pumpkin Pancakes 11
Pumpkin Seed Brittle 91
Pumpkin Waffles 18

Q

Quick And Easy Black Bean Soup 84
Quinoa And Red Lentil Stuffed Peppers With A Creamy Cashew Sauce 61
Quinoa And Spinach Power Salad 15
Quinoa With Mixed Vegetables And Cilantro Peanut Pesto 65

R

Raspberry Polenta Waffles 18
Ricotta Breakfast Toast Two Ways 17
Roast Beef Salad With Beets, Apple, And Horseradish 73
Roasted Beet Salad With Yogurt-dill Dressing 69
Roasted Salmon Fillets With Basil Drizzle 48
Roasted Steelhead Trout With Grapefruit Sauce 52

S

Salad Niçoise 68
Salmon Cakes 47
Scrambled Eggs With Apples, Sage, And Swiss Cheese 11
Sea Scallops And Vegetables With Ginger Sauce 49
Seafood Paella With Green Veg 56
Seasoned Turkey Burgers With Sautéed Mushrooms And Swiss 39
Shrimp With Corn Hash 51
Shrimp, Mango, And Black Bean Salad 74
Simple Autumn Salad 24
Sloppy Toms 45
Southwestern Bean-and-pepper Salad 21
Speedy Samosa Pasta 63
Spiced Roast Eye Of Round 29
Spicy Chicken Mac N Cheese 41
Spicy Sichuan Orange Beef Vegetable Stir-fry 33
Spicy Tilapia With Pineapple Relish 54
Spinach Burgers 60
Stir-fried Cabbage And Noodles 26
Strawberry Yogurt Smoothie 15
Stuffed Sweet Potatoes With Pistachios And Asparagus 25
Summer Salmon Parcels 53
Summer Veg Brekkie Cup 16
Summer Vegetable Risotto 59
Sweet & Sour Pork Chops 34

Made in the USA
Monee, IL
11 October 2023

44386773R00057